Puerto Rico

PUERTO RICO BY ROAD

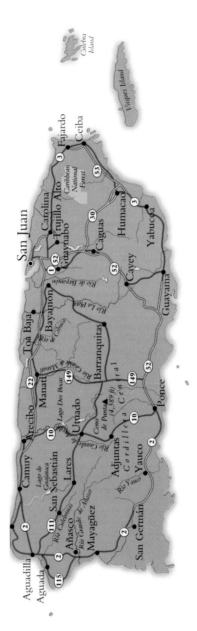

NATIONAL FOREST

0   5   10   15   20   25   30   35

MILES

Caribbean Sea

N
E
S
W

Celebrate the States

Puerto Rico

Martin Schwabacher and Steve Otfinoski

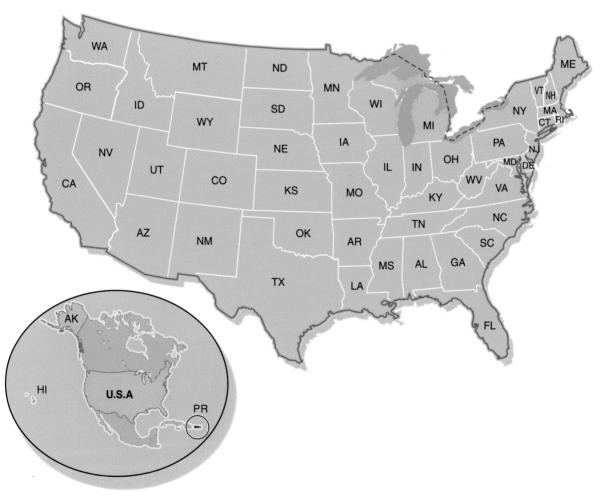

Marshall Cavendish
Benchmark
New York

Published by Marshall Cavendish Benchmark
An imprint of Marshall Cavendish Corporation

This publication represents the opinions and views of the authors based on Martin Schwabacher's and Steve Otfinoski's personal experiences, knowledge, and research. The information in this book serves as a general guide only. The authors and publisher have used their best efforts in preparing this book and disclaim liability rising directly and indirectly from the use and application of this book.

Other Marshall Cavendish Offices:
Marshall Cavendish Ltd. 5th Floor, 32-38 Saffron Hill, London EC1N 8 FH, UK • Marshall Cavendish International (Asia) Private Limited, 1 New Industrial Road, Singapore 536196 • Marshall Cavendish International (Thailand) Co Ltd. 253 Asoke, 12th Flr, Sukhumvit 21 Road, Klongtoey Nua, Wattana, Bangkok 10110, Thailand • Marshall Cavendish (Malaysia) Sdn Bhd, Times Subang, Lot 46, Subang Hi-Tech Industrial Park, Batu Tiga, 40000 Shah Alam, Selangor Darul Ehsan, Malaysia

Marshall Cavendish is a trademark of Times Publishing Limited

All websites were available and accurate when this book was sent to press.

Library of Congress Cataloging-in-Publication Data

Schwabacher, Martin.
Puerto Rico / by Martin Schwabacher and Steve Otfinoski.—2nd ed.
p. cm. — (Celebrate the states)
Summary: "Provides comprehensive information on the geography, history, wildlife, governmental structure, economy, cultural diversity, peoples, religion, and landmarks of Puerto Rico"—Provided by publisher.
Includes bibliographical references and index.
ISBN 978-0-7614-4734-4
1. Puerto Rico—Juvenile literature. I. Otfinoski, Steven. II. Title.

F1958.3.S39 2011
972.95—dc22
2009007066

Editor: Christine Florie
Co-Editor: Denise Pangia
Publisher: Michelle Bisson
Art Director: Anahid Hamparian
Series Designer: Adam Mietlowski

Photo research and layout by Marshall Cavendish International (Asia) Private Limited—
Thomas Khoo, Benson Tan and Gu Jing

Cover photo by Photolibrary

The photographs in this book are used by permission and through the courtesy of; *Corbis*: back cover, 20, 35, 37, 42, 44, 60, 65, 71, 82, 93, 94, 124, 128; *DK Images*: 24, 25, 27; *Getty Images*: 39, 45, 56, 64, 67, 117, 118, 121, 122, 123, 125, 126, 127; *Lonely Planet Images*: 48, 50; National Geographic Stock: 72; *Photolibrary*: 8, 10, 12, 13, 14, 19, 32, 47, 51, 53, 62, 75, 84, 85, 89, 91, 103, 107, 111, 115, 129; *Photolibrary/Alamy*: 15, 17, 22, 26, 52, 54, 59, 77, 79, 87, 90, 92, 96, 98, 100, 112, 130, 131, 132, 133, 135, 136; *Reuters*: 113; *Spectrum Photofile*: 103.

Printed in Malaysia
1 3 5 6 4 2

Contents

Puerto Rico Is . . .

Puerto Rico is a tropical island whose people are as warm to visitors as the climate.

"The culture embraced me like family and I played the best baseball of my professional career to that point . . . all while finding the most wonderful personal peace I had ever experienced."

—retired Major League Baseball outfielder Doug Glanville

Puerto Ricans have mixed feelings about being part of the United States . . .

"We stand as a nation surrounded by industry, but with little of it belonging to our people. . . . The United States controls our economy, our commerce . . . resulting in poverty for our people and wealth for the United States."

—nationalist leader Pedro Albizu Campos, 1937

"My parents saw the Americans come in. They knew what life was like before that. They were so grateful. There were no schools. It helped them."

—banker Marta Ramos

. . . and the United States has had mixed feelings about Puerto Rico.

"The United States is overdue in reengaging with this special place, which landed in our lap as a stepchild of imperialism in 1898, and which we have never seen clearly."

—Michael Janeway, professor of
journalism and art at Columbia University

Those that leave their homeland often miss it.

"I'm from the northeast coast of Puerto Rico, where you can see a beautiful beach in my backyard. Coming up here, you're stuck in between buildings and traffic."

—Catholic brother Juanmaria, who now lives in Bronx, New York

Their ancestors came from many places, but they are now one people— Puerto Ricans.

"The native Taíno Indians, the Spanish who conquered the island in the sixteenth century, the Africans brought here as slaves to work in the cane fields, the Americans who seized the reins of power from the Spanish in 1898, and recent immigrants from elsewhere in the Caribbean, notably Cuba, have all contributed mightily to the rich alloy of Puerto Rican life."

—journalist R. W. Apple Jr.

Puerto Rico is factories and palm trees, skyscrapers and remote mountain towns, universities and tropical rain forests. It is cars, coral, cliffs, and caves. Puerto Rico has been dominated by outsiders for centuries, ruled first by Spain, then by the United States. Though many Puerto Ricans are proud to be U.S. citizens, some have not given up the dream of having an independent country. Long before it was discovered by Christopher Columbus, Puerto Rico already had a name—the name used by the Taíno people who stood onshore to greet him. Five hundred years later many Puerto Ricans still prefer to use this name. To them, their island is Borinquen ("Island of the Brave Lord"), and they are Boricuas.

Chapter One

Mountain in the Sea

Puerto Rico is famous for its beautiful beaches, lush scenery, and warm climate. Located about 1,000 miles off the southern tip of Florida, it is a true tropical island. It is part of a long chain of islands that stretches from Florida to South America, separating the Caribbean Sea from the Atlantic Ocean.

Puerto Rico is just 33 miles wide and 100 miles long. If it were a state, it would rank forty-ninth in size, larger than only Delaware and Rhode Island. Yet on this small island live more than 3.8 million people, making it one of the most densely populated places on Earth.

A JAGGED LANDSCAPE

Puerto Rico is almost completely covered by hills and mountains. This terrain is not all gentle, rounded curves. Some of the mountains have jutting points, like a cloth draped over a pile of furniture. A ridge of tall mountains called the Cordillera Central (cor-dee-YEHR-a sen-TRAHL), the "central range," stretches down the middle of the island from east to west. The Luquillo (loo-KEE-yo) Mountains guard the island's eastern tip.

The island of Puerto Rico is centrally located in the arc of submerged mountains that connects North America with South America and forms the archipelago of the Antilles.

Cordillera Central, the main mountain range in Puerto Rico, crosses the island from west to east with an elevation of 3,000 feet and divides the territory's northern and southern coastal plains.

Some of the most unusual mountains are located in the northwest, in karst country. Karst is created when parts of the ground collapse, leaving odd, lumpy shapes. This happens when water flowing underground dissolves the limestone rock.

Flat, narrow strips of land run along the island's north and south coasts. Puerto Rico's famous sandy beaches are located in these areas, along with most of the island's big cities. On the island's eastern and western tips the hills drop down into the sea, forming lowlands and beaches.

LAND AND WATER

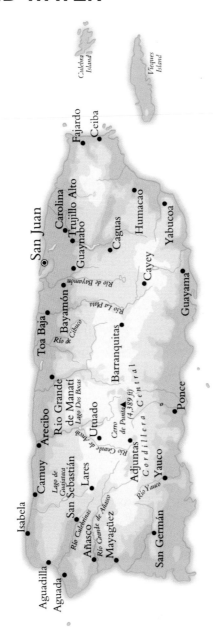

ATLANTIC OCEAN

Caribbean Sea

Culebra Island

Vieques Island

Fajardo
Ceiba

Carolina
Trujillo Alto
Guaynabo
Humacao
Caguas
Yabucoa
San Juan
Cayey
Río de Bayamón
Guayama
Toa Baja
Bayamón
Río La Plata
Río de Chuco
Barranquitas
Río Grande de Manatí
Cordillera Central
Río de las Bocas
Lago Dos Bocas
Utuado
Arecibo
Cerro de Punta (4,389 ft)
Ponce
Río Grande de Arecibo
Camuy
Lago de Guajataca
San Sebastián
Adjuntas
Lares
Yauco
Río Culebrinas
Río Yauco
Isabela
Añasco
Mayagüez
Río Grande de Añasco
San Germán
Aguadilla
Aguada

3,000 – 6,000 ft.
1,500 – 3,000 ft.
600 – 1,500 ft.
300 – 600 ft.
0 – 300 ft.

0 5 10 15 20 25 30
MILES

N
E
S
W

Mona Island

Offshore, Puerto Rico is rich in coral reefs—colorful, jagged structures built over thousands of years by tiny sea creatures. Coral reefs are a favorite haven for tropical fish, which makes them a great place for scuba diving and snorkeling.

Some of the best places to see coral are the smaller offshore islands that are part of Puerto Rico. Seven miles to the east is Puerto Rico's largest offshore island, Vieques, where coral can be found near the beach. A less developed and populated island, Culebra, is nearby. Parts of Culebra and twenty-three smaller islands are protected as the Culebra National Wildlife Refuge. They are home to large colonies of nesting birds, along with endangered leatherback and hawksbill turtles.

To the west of the main island is Mona Island, which is surrounded by beautiful coral reefs. No one lives on Mona now, but it was once a hideout for pirates, and there are rumors that pirate treasure is still hidden somewhere in Mona's network of caves.

Mona Island is just one of the many small islands that surround Puerto Rico.

ENDANGERED LEATHERBACK

Tired of always doing the same old things at the beach? On your next vacation, try something different—like rescuing a baby leatherback sea turtle.

The leatherback is the only turtle without a hard shell. Instead, it has a leathery cover. Leatherbacks can grow to be more than 6 feet long and can weigh almost 2,000 pounds. They are one of the largest living reptiles; only three kinds of crocodiles and alligators are bigger. With their enormous flippers, leatherbacks can swim thousands of miles through the open ocean, but they must come onto the beach to nest.

The Puerto Rican island of Culebra is a key nesting area for leatherbacks. A female leatherback crawls onshore, digs a hole, and lays her eggs. Seven weeks later the babies hatch and scramble down the beach into the ocean.

The presence of people has made life difficult for leatherbacks. Electric lights confuse the baby turtles and cause them to crawl in the wrong direction. Construction and pollution destroy their nesting grounds. Some turtles are killed by boats. Others swallow plastic objects or get tangled in fishing nets and die.

In 1970 leatherback turtles were declared endangered. To help keep their population from declining, volunteers search the beaches of Culebra for turtle hatchlings each night from April through August. They guard the babies and make sure they find their way into the water. "It was super fun," recalled volunteer Lori Applebaum. "We had to go barefoot, because you don't want to accidentally step on them. We went out after dark with flashlights and pointed the way to the water so the baby turtles could find their way."

Puerto Rico is home to about 270 kinds of birds. Some, such as the Puerto Rican emerald hummingbird and the Adelaide's warbler, live only in Puerto Rico. Many of Puerto Rico's most common birds, such as the Puerto Rican bullfinch and the stripe-headed tanager, eat the island's abundant fruit. The Puerto Rican flycatcher, the Puerto Rican woodpecker, and many other birds feed on insects. The Puerto Rican lizard cuckoo hops from tree branch to tree branch, snatching up lizards, while terns, coots, and herons feed in the water. Puerto Rico's two most famous birds are the guaraguao, a red-tail hawk and bird of prey, and the pitirre, also known as the gray kingbird. Because of its aggressive defense of its territory, the pitirre has become a symbol of the Puerto Rican independence movement.

One of the island's rarest birds is the Puerto Rican parrot. Before Europeans arrived on the island, Puerto Rico was completely covered with trees. Back then about a million of these bright green birds nested in holes in tree trunks. Now most of the trees are gone, along with the parrots. In 1975 only thirteen remained. Today, breeding programs have increased the population to two hundred.

Close to extinction only a few decades ago, the Puerto Rican parrot is making a comeback.

There are even more lizards than birds in Puerto Rico. Wherever you look, in the city or the country, you are likely to see a lizard. They come in many colors: brown, green, tan, speckled, or striped like a zebra. The largest of Puerto Rico's lizards is the rock iguana, which lives on Mona Island. It grows to be more than 3 feet long. The smallest, called sphaeros, can be as small as 1.5 inches when fully grown—including their tails. The lizards you are most likely to see are anoles, which come in many colors. If you look closely, they can be found sitting on leaves and tree trunks just about everywhere.

The Caribbean rock iguana is native to Mona Island and is the largest land lizard in Puerto Rico.

Puerto Rico's most beloved animal is a tiny frog called the coquí. Coquís are about 1 inch long, live in trees, and sing with a delightful sweet tone. Puerto Rico has sixteen varieties of coquís. Some click, others warble, but the most common noise is a two-note call that sounds just like its name: co-KEE, co-KEE. Each evening the coquís' cheerful songs can be heard across the island. "The coquí is very noisy, but it helps me sleep," says one boy.

There are almost no large mammals on Puerto Rico. This is not so surprising when you think of the great distance between it and the mainland of North and South America. Seeds of plants and trees could be carried to Puerto Rico by birds, could float there on ocean waves, or could blow there in the wind. Lizards could float to the island on logs. But there was no easy way for larger animals to travel there from the mainland.

Among the few mammals that made the long trip on their own were bats, because unlike other mammals, they have wings. Thirteen kinds of bats now live on Puerto Rico, ranging from small ones that eat insects and fruit to the larger bulldog bat, which has a 2-foot wingspan and catches fish for food. Bats, like birds, help the environment by gobbling up insects and spreading the seeds of fruit trees around the forest through their waste. The island's large wild mammal, the mongoose, was brought there by Europeans to kill rats on sugarcane plantations.

BLAZING COLORS

Puerto Rico's real attraction for wilderness lovers is its dazzling plant life. Flowers that elsewhere would require careful nurturing in a greenhouse grow naturally in the hot, humid climate. Bright flowers such as orchids, bougainvillea, jasmine, and hibiscus grow everywhere.

A favorite tree is the flamboyant, or flame tree, which is lit up by a blaze of orange-red blossoms that makes it appear as if it is on fire. Other unusual trees include the ausubo, which has wood so hard that it is virtually indestructible, and the ceiba, whose aboveground roots look like a tangle of octopus tentacles. In all, there are 547 species of trees native to Puerto Rico.

Though Puerto Rico's travel posters always show a beach with white sand, some parts of the shoreline are crowded instead with mangrove trees. These trees shelter much wildlife in their tangled roots. Oysters, lobsters, birds, and sometimes even blubbery, whalelike mammals called manatees feed there.

In Culebra Island the flamboyant tree shows off its glowing orange-red flowers during June through July.

One of the most popular fish for anglers in Puerto Rico is the huge marlin. But other fish abound, from colorful tropical fish often seen in aquariums to hefty red snappers and tuna.

ENDLESS SUMMER

Nearly 5 million people travel to Puerto Rico each year to enjoy its endless summer. The average high temperature in San Juan is 80 degrees Fahrenheit in January and 84 °F in July. It never snows in Puerto Rico—the coldest temperature ever recorded there is 39 °F. Though the mountains are usually cooler, the coastal cities can be hot and humid. On steamy days, says Basilio Graciani Peña, a San Juan cabdriver, "Even when it rains, you sweat." The air is so muggy, "It's like flan in your face." (Flan is thick, sticky custard, a favorite Puerto Rican dessert.)

Because the temperature hardly changes throughout the year in Puerto Rico, the seawater always stays at about 81 °F. But its slightly cooler temperature in winter is enough to keep Puerto Ricans from swimming in the sea. "I would never go into the water in December. It's too cold," says Roberto Prado of Ponce. "But when tourists come down here from the States, they jump right in. For them it's like chicken broth."

CATCHING CLOUDS

Puerto Rico gets a steady stream of air currents from the northeast called the trade winds, which sailors once took advantage of to propel their ships. These winds bring clouds of warm, moist ocean air to the island. As the clouds reach Puerto Rico, they hit the Luquillo Mountains on Puerto Rico's eastern tip. As a result, it rains there almost every day, creating a lush tropical rain forest. This region has been preserved as the Caribbean National Forest, the only tropical rain forest in the U.S. national park system.

All the mountains on the island receive abundant rain. Because the land gets warmer than the ocean, the air over the island heats up. Hot air rises, so moist air is continually drawn up the mountainsides, creating towers of rain clouds. Clouds pile up over the mountains, erupting in thunderstorms even when it is sunny at the beach.

Since clouds usually approach the island from the northeast, there is a cloud "shadow" on the southwestern side of the island. On this side of the mountains it is so dry that instead of lush green, you'll find a lot of cactuses and gnarly trees clinging to the bare rocks.

El Yunque National Forest is the only tropical rain forest in the U.S. National Forest System.

Hurricane Georges was the first hurricane to cross the entire island since the San Ciprian Hurricane in 1932.

HURRICANE LANE

Though Puerto Rico is blessed with natural beauty and a pleasant climate, nature does present one major menace: hurricanes. Puerto Rico is often directly in the path of these huge storms, which regularly sweep through the Caribbean. Their powerful winds can blow up to 200 miles per hour.

Hurricane season lasts from June to November. During August the excitement and anxiety is at its peak. When a big hurricane hits, it can cause hundreds of millions of dollars in damage. After Hurricane Georges, in 1998, "We went thirty-two days without power," says a resident of Bayamón. "My father didn't have any power or water for three months." Many people store water in containers on their roofs and buy home generators for their refrigerators, just in case. But some things money can't replace. After Hurricane Hugo struck in 1989, one Puerto Rican recalled, "There were no leaves on the trees." People especially mourned the loss of the singing coquís that were washed away from their gardens.

Though people often lose water and power to hurricanes, few worry about losing their homes. That's because most houses on Puerto Rico are made of concrete. The thick, boxlike structures can withstand just about anything. A few of these houses don't even have glass in the windows. They just let the breezes blow through the shutters. When you live somewhere as beautiful as Puerto Rico, a cool breeze on a hot day is enough to make life seems pretty good.

Chapter Two

Centuries of Struggle

In 1493 Christopher Columbus became the first European to reach Puerto Rico. But he was not the first person to discover the island. For the people already living on Puerto Rico, Columbus's journey meant not a new beginning but the end of their way of life.

BEFORE COLUMBUS

The first people to reach Puerto Rico probably came by raft or canoe from the Yucatán Peninsula in Mexico. This peninsula juts out toward Cuba, the largest of a string of islands called the Antilles, which stretch from Florida to South America.

Around 2000 BCE the Ortoiroid people from South America began working their way up the Antilles to Puerto Rico. They settled on the coast, where they lived by fishing and gathering food and made tools from bone, shell, and stone. Another group called the Igneri, from South America, arrived between 1200 BCE and 400 CE. They hunted with bows and arrows and slept in hammocks at night. They also made pottery and grew such crops as corn and sweet potatoes, which they had brought with them from South America.

Many of the central buildings in the city and harbor of Ponce, Puerto Rico, were erected between the late 1890s and the 1930s.

The Taínos culture developed out of this group. By about 1000 CE they settled the entire island. The Taínos lived in villages of more than a thousand people that were led by chiefs called caciques (kah SEE kess), who could be either male or female. They lived in large round buildings, made of wood with thatched roofs, that were shared by several families. Each Taíno village had at least one ball court, in which the people played a game that involved bouncing a rubber ball without using the hands or feet. Early Spanish explorers

The cacique of the Taínos is carried on a raised platform by his tribesmen. The club that he holds is a symbol of his power.

said the courts were never empty. The Spaniards had never seen rubber before and were astounded at how high the ball bounced.

The Taíno were of average height for this time period, the men usually just over 5 feet tall. They had high cheekbones, dark eyes, and olive or copper skin. They traveled between Puerto Rico and other islands in canoes carved from single logs. Some canoes could hold eighty people. The Taíno were skilled farmers who grew such foods as cassava and sweet potatoes. The starchy roots of the yucca were ground and baked into bread. Corn, beans, and squash were all introduced to the Europeans by the Taíno. Fish and reptiles were also important in the Taíno diet.

THE FRIENDLIEST PEOPLE IN THE WORLD

A new wave of settlement in the Caribbean began in 1492, when the Italian explorer Christopher Columbus sailed across the Atlantic in hopes of discovering a new route from Europe to Asia. Instead, he stumbled upon the Americas, although he thought he had reached the outer rim of the East. The news caused a sensation in Spain. The royal family, who had sponsored his trip, immediately sent Columbus back. On November 19, 1493, he landed on Puerto Rico. Columbus found a thriving island inhabited by as many as 50,000 Taíno. He received a friendly welcome.

Explorer Christopher Columbus meets Taíno tribesmen in their village after landing on Puerto Rico during his second voyage to the New World.

Columbus called the island San Juan Bautista ("Saint John the Baptist" in Spanish). Fifteen years after Columbus's visit, a new representative of the Spanish crown, Juan Ponce de León, arrived. He established the island's first Spanish settlement, Caparra, on its eastern part, which was later moved and became known as San Juan.

On first seeing the large bay, Ponce de León supposedly cried "Que puerto rico!" which is Spanish for "What a rich port!" In 1521 Puerto Rico replaced San Juan Bautista as the name of the entire island.

Ponce de León's job was to turn the island into a colony—a place ruled and used by a foreign power. "There

Juan Ponce de León was Puerto Rico's first Spanish governor and one of the Spanish colony's founding fathers.

will be no problem, your highness," he wrote back to the king. "These are the friendliest people in the world." Though fewer in number, the Spaniards had better weapons than the Taíno. They soon enslaved many of the Taíno and forced them to search for gold. The Taíno rebelled in 1511 but were quickly defeated by the Spaniards. Within fifteen years of the Europeans' arrival, most of the Taíno had died from starvation or disease. About the only Taíno left were those who had escaped the European settlements by fleeing into the mountains.

Taíno uprisings were put down harshly by the Spanish.

SLAVERY AND WAR

The Spaniards divided the island into farms, including a few large ones, called plantations, where they grew primarily sugarcane, but also such crops as ginger and tobacco. In 1513 they began importing slaves from Africa to work in the fields. By the mid–1500s, however, the Puerto Rican sugar industry had fallen behind that of neighboring islands. By the end of the century ginger replaced sugar as the colony's main cash crop. For the next two hundred years Puerto Rico was mostly used as a Spanish military outpost.

Over the years San Juan suffered many attacks. In 1595 the Spaniards barely fought off the English pirate Sir Frances Drake. Three years later, when Spanish troops were weakened by dysentery, George Clifford, the English Earl of Cumberland, captured San Juan. The same illness then struck the English. After six hundred English troops died in six weeks, Cumberland withdrew. Then in 1625 Dutch invaders laid siege to San Juan and burned much of the city. But these were merely brief interruptions in a period of Spanish rule that would last four centuries.

EL AZUCARERO
(THE SUGARCANE WORKER)

Though harvesting sugarcane is backbreaking work, in this song the worker takes pride in the fruit of his labor.

Sem - bre - mos ca - ña de a - zu - car en la
We're plant - ing the canes of su - gar, 'Neath the

zo - na tro - pi - cal. Que hay en el res - to del
burn - ing tro - pic skies. Be - cause the world has much that's

mun - do mu - chas co - sas que en dul - zar.
bit - ter, And for sweet - en - ing it cries.

Fine

Allí está el azucarero,
Cual abeja colossal,
Que en provecho de nosotros
Va formando su panal.

Chorus

See! There stands the sugar worker,
Like a great and skillful bee,
Forming, with his work, the beehive
That provides for you and me.

THE JÍBAROS

While the Spaniards used the best farmland along the coasts for plantations, independent peasants called *jíbaros* (HEE-ba-rohs) survived on small farms in the mountains. Some were runaway slaves and others were of mixed race—the children of Spanish immigrants, Taíno, and escaped African slaves. Their mountain farms were so remote and isolated that they had little direct contact with the Spanish authorities or the Catholic Church.

The popular image of the jíbaro is of a proud, self-reliant farmer with a straw hat and a large knife called a machete. The jíbaro still symbolizes freedom and independence to Puerto Ricans, much like the cowboy represents the spirit of the American West in the United States. Jíbaro traditions, such as taking in travelers and helping neighbors through hard times, live on in Puerto Rico today.

UNDER THE YOKE

By the early 1800s the Spaniards were turning more and more land into large plantations. A law passed in 1848 required anyone who did not own land to work for a large landowner. This policy was designed to turn the independent jíbaros into plantation laborers. Unemployment was a crime punishable by jail sentences or beatings.

Also starting in 1848 all farm workers were required to carry a black book called a *libreta*. Anyone punished for disobedience received a black mark in his libreta. A worker with a black mark often could not find work. These hated books also contained records of debts the workers could not repay, which kept them tied to the large plantation owners like slaves.

By this time the island's landowners and business owners were growing unhappy under Spanish rule. They paid heavy taxes to the king and were barred from trading with any country but Spain—a law they often ignored. Eventually a nationalist movement arose, seeking independence from Spain. Its leader was Ramón Emeterio Betances, who had studied medicine in France and returned to care for the island's poor. Betances denounced Spanish rule, writing, "We have been paying immense taxes and still have no roads, railways, telegraph systems, and steamships. The rabble of Spain—soldiers and clerks—come to Puerto Rico and squeeze us dry, returning to their homeland with millions belonging to us. The government prohibits schools, newspapers, and books."

Betances organized a rebellion against the Spanish forces. A government spy discovered the secret plan, and several nationalist leaders were arrested. But the revolt took place anyway. Rebels captured the town of Lares on September 23, 1868, and announced the creation of the Republic of Puerto Rico. Though the rebellion was quickly crushed, this day is still commemorated in Puerto Rico. It is known as El Grito de Lares—the shout of Lares—and symbolizes the Puerto Rican people's long-simmering desire to be independent.

In 1897 a new government in Spain allowed Puerto Ricans partial self-rule. Puerto Rico was declared a self-governing state. It would have an elected congress that shared power with a governor from Spain. Puerto Rico's new government took control in July 1898, but it was short-lived.

The United States wanted to force Spain out of the Caribbean, and war broke out between the nations. Less than a month after the new government had formed, U.S. troops landed at Guánica, Puerto Rico, on July 25, 1898. They met with little resistance from the Spanish army, and the Spanish-American War was soon over. After four centuries of Spanish domination, Puerto Ricans found themselves with a new colonial ruler, the United States.

U.S. troops victoriously enter Ponce during the Spanish-American War of 1898, which brought an end to Spanish colonial rule.

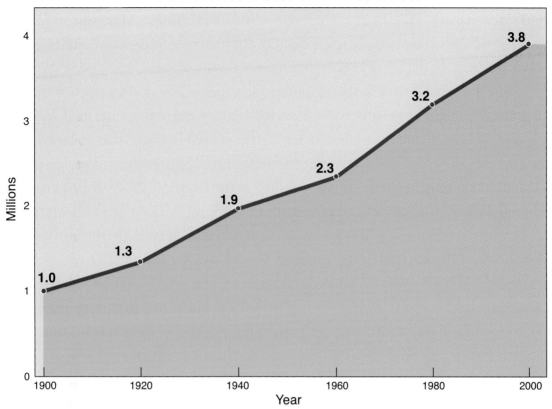

POPULATION GROWTH: 1900–2000

Millions

- 1.0 (1900)
- 1.3 (1920)
- 1.9 (1940)
- 2.3 (1960)
- 3.2 (1980)
- 3.8 (2000)

Year

AMERICAN RULE

"We have come . . . to promote your prosperity and bestow upon you the . . . blessing of the liberal institutions of our government," announced the conquering U.S. general, Nelson Miles. Preferring independence to such blessings, Betances angrily predicted that "If Puerto Rico does not act fast, it will be an American colony forever." Both were partly right. American rule brought many improvements, but more than a hundred years later, Puerto Rico still would not be independent.

When the United States took over, only one out of ten children attended school. Health and education improved under American rule. New roads and electric lines spanned the island, and many schools were built.

The Foraker Act of 1900, a federal law passed by Congress, set up a limited civilian government in Puerto Rico. It created a Puerto Rican elected house of delegates, but it had little power because the governor and an executive council were appointed by the U.S. president. The Jones Act of 1917, another federal law, made Puerto Ricans U.S. citizens, and changed the island's system of government, making it more like U.S. state governments. Some 18,000 of these new citizens served in the armed forces when the United States entered World War I that same year.

After World War I ended, American businesses such as the Amalgamated Sugar Company bought the best farmland in Puerto Rico. While some jíbaros still ran their own farms in the mountains, most Puerto Ricans worked for foreigners under harsh conditions. One man who worked for Amalgamated Sugar remembered, "If we stopped work to rest a moment, they would come and spit on us and kick us, beat us with barber straps."

THE FIGHT FOR SELF-GOVERNMENT

In the 1930s a new nationalist movement arose under a lawyer named Pedro Albizu Campos. He argued that Puerto Rico was a free state when it was invaded by the United States, and that the two countries were still at war. During a nationalist rally at the University of Puerto Rico in 1935, several demonstrators were killed. Two nationalists retaliated by shooting the police chief. The killers were arrested and

Pedro Albizu Campos was one of the leading figures in the Puerto Rican independence movement during the 1930s.

beaten to death, and Albizu Campos and seven other nationalist leaders were sent to prison. Protests continued, and during a peaceful demonstration in Ponce in 1937, Puerto Rican police killed nineteen nationalist demonstrators and wounded one hundred more in what is now known as the Ponce Massacre.

Albizu Campos was released from prison ten years later and found the movement still alive. In 1950 nationalists stormed the police station in San Juan, the town hall in Mayagüez, and the mayor's office in Lares. A revolt in the town of Jayuya resulted in a counterattack by U.S. bomber planes and land artillery. That same year two armed Puerto Rican nationalists attacked the residence of U.S. president Harry Truman, and in 1954 nationalists entered the U.S. House of Representatives and shot and wounded five congressmen.

But no matter how passionate the nationalists were, they never received widespread backing from the Puerto Rican people. Most people had thrown their support behind a more moderate leader, Luis Muñoz Marín. Early in his career Muñoz Marín supported full independence, but later he came to believe that the best way to improve Puerto Rico was to work with the United States, not against it.

Muñoz Marín started the Popular Democratic Party, known by its Spanish initials as the PPD. The PPD appealed to working people with the slogan *Pan, Tierra, y Libertad* (Bread, Land, and Liberty) and offered them rent-free government land. In 1948, when Puerto Ricans were allowed to elect their governor themselves for the first time, they overwhelmingly chose Muñoz Marín.

By this time Muñoz Marín had backed away from seeking independence in favor of a compromise. Puerto Rico would have its own government, but it would remain part of the United States as a commonwealth. Puerto Ricans voted in favor of the new status in 1951, and their new constitution went into effect in 1952.

The Puerto Rican Legislative Assembly enters its final session of the Constitutional Assembly, approving the island's first constitution in its five-century history.

Muñoz Marín and the U.S. Congress came up with a plan to develop Puerto Rico's economy. Known as Operation Bootstrap, the plan called for U.S. companies to build factories on the island to employ Puerto Rican workers. In return the businesses would pay no taxes for seventeen years and would receive other incentives.

From 1947 to 1960 the number of factories in Puerto Rico increased enormously. By 1955 manufacturing was a bigger part of the island's economy than agriculture. Hospitals and schools were built, teachers and doctors were trained, and highways and houses were constructed.

Though U.S. president Dwight Eisenhower called it "the single most impressive plan of economic development in the free world," Operation Bootstrap did not come close to employing all of Puerto Rico's people. Thousands of people moved from the countryside to the cities in search of jobs that didn't exist.

To ease unemployment, the Puerto Rican and U.S. governments urged people to move to the United States. As Muñoz Marín put it, "Our problem was there weren't enough jobs for the people and we couldn't bring the jobs in fast enough. Some people had to leave." Billboards urged people to move to New York City, and the government helped pay their way. Large Puerto Rican communities sprang up in New York and other cities.

But even a massive migration that would bring more than a million Puerto Ricans to the mainland was not enough to ease the unemployment problem. One controversial method the government used to control the population was to give women operations that made it impossible for them to have more children. Some women were asked to agree to the operation right after giving birth. Many did not understand that it was permanent. By 1965 a third of all Puerto Rican women of childbearing age had been sterilized.

Pollution was another negative result of Operation Bootstrap. Oil and chemical plants along the south coast caused diseases that have shortened residents' life spans in some areas by ten years. Pollution and overfishing ruined the island's fishing industry. In the 1960s, 4,000 pounds of fish were caught in the Manatí River each year. But the river became so polluted by American drug factories that by 1976, only 40 pounds of fish were caught in the river's brown, smelly water. Despite a natural bounty that could once feed its people five times over, Puerto Rico now must import almost all of its food from the mainland.

Oil refineries created jobs in Puerto Rico, but also created widespread pollution that affected residents' health.

THE BATTLE FOR VIEQUES

For more than sixty years the U.S. Navy had been conducting bombing exercises on a 900-acre firing range on the eastern tip of the Puerto Rican island of Vieques. Many of the nine thousand people who live on Vieques had been unhappy with the bombing for decades and wanted it to stop. The navy refused to listen to their complaints that the bombing was potentially dangerous to residents. Then in April 1999 a local security guard was killed by a bomb that missed its target. Protests and demonstrations against the bombing escalated, often involving Puerto Rican and mainland celebrities, including actors and writers.

Finally, in June 2001, U.S. president George W. Bush announced that the bombing exercises would end. The navy left Vieques in May 2003. Then-governor Sila M. Calderón called the navy's departure "the beginning of a new era of peace and tranquility" for Vieques. The U.S. Department of the Interior provided funding to clean up the bombing site and transform it into a wildlife refuge. In 2009 residents expressed new concerns about the release of contaminants as the navy proposed to burn 100 acres of vegetation in order to locate and detonate long-hidden cluster bombs on the site.

PASSIONATE DEBATE

The debate over whether to tighten or loosen the island's ties to the United States continues to dominate Puerto Rican politics. Puerto Rico is poorer than any of the fifty U.S. states. But Puerto Ricans are better off than their Caribbean neighbors, thanks in part to American investment and industry. Though Puerto Ricans are proud and independent-minded, few want to face the uncertain economic future that would come with independence.

In 1968 the New Progressive Party (PNP) was formed to promote the idea that Puerto Rico should become the fifty-first U.S. state. Since then the PNP has exchanged power with the PPD several times.

In a referendum vote held in 1998, about 46 percent of Puerto Ricans voted in favor of statehood. But the debate continues. In December 2005 a presidential task force recommended a two-step process to decide the question. In the first step Puerto Ricans would vote on whether they wanted a permanent resolution of their status. If they voted in favor of a resolution, they would then vote for either independence or statehood. As of 2009 this recommendation has not been acted on. Puerto Rico's new governor, Luis G. Fortuño, elected in November 2008, supports statehood.

Chapter Three

Island Life

Puerto Ricans pride themselves on having their own cultural traditions that are separate from those of the United States. Their mixed feelings about being connected to the United States are shown in their views toward the island's official language. Spanish and English had both been official languages since 1902, but in 1991, the government made Spanish the only official language. Then in 1993 Governor Pedro J. Rossello restored English to equal status with Spanish.

While virtually all Puerto Ricans are Hispanic, immigration in recent years has added more ethnic groups to the Puerto Rican melting pot. According to the 2000 Census whites made up 83 percent of Puerto Rico's population; African Americans, 8.3 percent; Americans Indians; 2 percent, and Asian, 1.1 percent.

TAÍNO—RETURN OF A NATIVE PEOPLE

Puerto Rico's last indigenous people, the Taíno, were virtually wiped out by the early Spanish explorers and colonists. But since the 1960s some Puerto Ricans have been working to reconnect with their American-

Puerto Ricans are proud of their unique culture.

Indian heritage. In 2003 geneticist Juan Martínez Cruzado conducted experiments that showed that 61 percent of Puerto Ricans have some Taíno DNA in their bodies.

The unearthing of Taíno artifacts has become a major goal of local archaeologists and museums. "The Indian heritage is very important because it united the Puerto Rican community," says archaeologist Miguel Rodríguez López. "There is a feeling that it represents our primary roots."

These vivid pictographs on stones in Utuado are among the largest of Taíno artifacts.

Since 1969 the mountain town of Jayuya, named after a Taíno chief, has held an annual National Indigenous Festival. The festival's climax is a beauty contest in which children ages six to sixteen dress in traditional Taíno costumes.

THE CHINESE

Chinese immigrants have been coming to Puerto Rico since the 1940s. Cuba also has a great number of Chinese immigrants. When Cuban dictator Fidel Castro came to power in 1959, most Cuban Chinese immigrated to Puerto Rico and the mainland United States. Some Chinese have intermarried with Puerto Ricans and have adopted Hispanic last names. Among the most famous Puerto Rican–Chinese are actor Kirk Acevedo, who starred in the television drama series *Oz*; and Christopher Moy, a member of the teen rock band Menudo.

The illegal immigration of Chinese nationals is a growing problem in Puerto Rico. Some of these illegals are brought into Puerto Rico and the Dominican Republic and then smuggled into the mainland United States.

Chinese-Puerto Rican Christopher Moy, born in Bronx, New York, sang for the teen rock band Menudo and more recently joined the band One Call.

ETHNIC PUERTO RICO

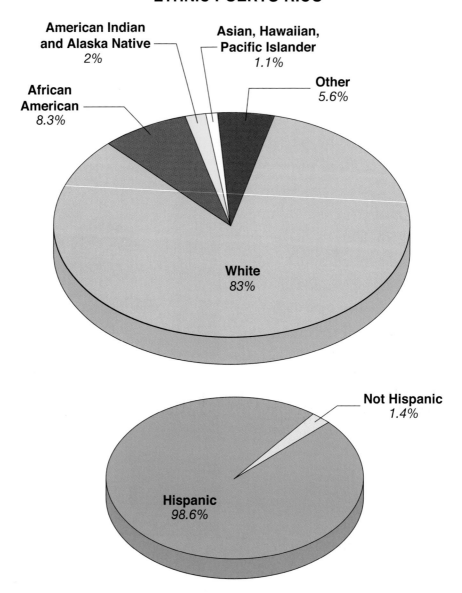

American Indian
and Alaska Native
2%

Asian, Hawaiian,
Pacific Islander
1.1%

Other
5.6%

African
American
8.3%

White
83%

Not Hispanic
1.4%

Hispanic
98.6%

Note: A person of Cuban, Mexican, Puerto Rican, South or Central American, or other Spanish culture or origin, regardless of race, is defined as Hispanic.

FRIENDS AND FAMILY

One tradition all Puerto Ricans take special pride in is friendliness and hospitality toward strangers. Someone you've just met for the first time might tell you, "If you ever come back, remember, you have another house."

Family is important to Puerto Ricans, who often have roots in a community that go back several generations. One person with relatives in the small town of Yabucoa says, "My mother has fourteen brothers and sisters, and except for one, everyone stayed in that town. You can imagine how many cousins I have." Though she moved to New York, she knows she always has a home in Puerto Rico.

These family ties often go beyond close relatives. Years ago children were often sent to live with relatives or close friends. Even today, community ties are stronger in Puerto Rico than in the United States. According to a schoolteacher who moved to San Juan from the United States, "When you ask for help, you will have it."

The family is a central focus in Puerto Rican life.

COOKING WITH LOVE

If a friend introduces you to his relatives, expect to be asked to dinner. "Never say no if they offer you food," cautions one Puerto Rican. Not only would it be considered rude to refuse, but you would miss a great meal. Simple foods like chicken just taste better in Puerto Rico. "Puerto Rican chicken is the best in the world. Pork—you can't get pork like Puerto Rican pork. It's outrageous!" raves Roberto Prado, a hotel owner in Ponce who cooks for his guests himself. Although much of the food in Puerto Rico is now imported, small farms and family plots still produce local foods such as bananas, mangoes, avocados, and chickens. There are no chickens fresher than the ones people raise for themselves.

Puerto Rican cuisine should not be confused with Mexican cuisine. You can find a dish called a *taco*, but in Puerto Rico it is a soft piece of fried dough stuffed with seafood or beef, not a Mexican-style taco. Instead of spicy chili peppers, Puerto Ricans cook with savory seasoning mixes like adobo and *sofrito*. Meats are sometimes barbecued, as they have been for centuries.

Mofongo, a dish made of fried plantains, garlic, and pork rinds, is a Puerto Rican specialty.

In fact, the word "barbecue" comes from the Taíno word *barbacoa*, their word for a rack that holds meat over a fire.

BARBECUED CHICKEN WITH ADOBO

This recipe combines three Puerto Rican favorites: chicken, barbecue, and adobo. In this recipe, the adobo seasoning makes a tasty barbecue sauce. Have an adult help you with the cooking.

2–3 pounds small chicken parts
juice of 1/2 a lime
2 tablespoons vegetable oil
adobo (see recipe below)

adobo
3 tablespoons vegetable oil
1 teaspoon chili powder
1/2 teaspoon garlic powder
1/2 teaspoon onion powder
1/2 teaspoon ground oregano
1 teaspoon salt
1/2 teaspoon black pepper
6 ounces tomato paste
juice of 1/2 a lime

Mix all the adobo ingredients thoroughly. Rub the chicken parts in the juice from half a lime. Spread the vegetable oil lightly over the chicken.

Turn on the oven's broiler. Place the chicken parts skin side–down in the broiler, and cook for twelve minutes, or until brown. Turn the chicken over and broil for eight more minutes, or until brown. Remove the chicken from the oven, and spread adobo on both sides. Put the chicken back into the broiler and cook until the adobo starts to char, about five minutes. You can also barbecue the chicken on a charcoal grill and use the adobo as barbecue sauce. Delicious!

One of the most popular local foods is the plantain, which looks like a giant banana. The yellow ones are sweet, and the green ones taste more like potato. Plantains can be cooked in several ways. You can fry slices of green plantains in oil to make *tostones*. You can mash these fried pieces with garlic and pork rinds to make *mofongo*. Served with chicken or shrimp, mofongo makes one of the heartiest meals you can eat. Another satisfying meal is the stew called *asopao*. You can't go wrong eating chicken, rice, and beans in Puerto Rico. As one cook put it, "When you're cooking, the first thing you put in the pan is your heart. After that, it doesn't matter what you put in."

Plantains, being prepared in a restaurant in Piñones, is an all-purpose food in Puerto Rico.

MUSIC AND CELEBRATION

Puerto Ricans enjoy many kinds of music, from classical to salsa to reggae to rap. The popular music styles heard most often on the radio are salsa and merengue, dance music filled with complex, fast-paced rhythms. Delia Morales, a mother with grown children, keeps the radio turned to a salsa station. "On Sundays we usually go dancing. There are a lot of places with music on the beach," she says. "And you dance, you have a wonderful time."

Music can be heard everywhere in Puerto Rico. These musicians are performing in San Juan's Old Town.

Salsa means "sauce" in Spanish, and according to the legendary drummer and bandleader Tito Puente, salsa is a mixture of "all our fast Latin music put together." Salsa emerged in New York, where Cuban and Puerto Rican musicians played with jazz musicians, mixing in rhythms brought to the Caribbean by enslaved Africans hundreds of years ago.

Other musical traditions go back even further. Instruments such as maracas, which make a rattling sound when shaken, were played by the Taíno. Stringed instruments like the cuatro were adapted from Spanish guitars and are still used today.

Any weekend is a time to socialize in Puerto Rico, but what really makes a Puerto Rican town come alive is a festival. Each year, every town has a festival honoring its patron saint. It usually lasts more than a week,

Colorful parades, such as this one in San Juan, are a highlight of the Christmas season.

and by the final weekend, the town plaza is filled with music, dancing, and stalls selling tasty food. A wooden statue of the saint is paraded through town on the final Sunday. Each town has its own traditions relating to local history or legends. In San Juan residents honor their patron saint, John the Baptist, by walking backward into the sea on the stroke of midnight, which is supposed to bring good luck for the coming year. In some cities, like Ponce and Loíza, the fiestas become carnivals filled with people wearing elaborate costumes.

Christmastime in Puerto Rico is the longest celebration of the year, lasting three weeks. Before the last day of Christmastime, January 6, Three Kings Day, children put boxes of grass under their beds for the kings' camels to eat. The next day the grass is gone, and the boxes are filled with presents.

EDUCATION

Education is a priority in Puerto Rico today, and all children must attend school from ages five through eighteen. Still many students drop out before finishing their secondary schooling. In 2000, 60 percent of all adult Puerto Ricans had received a high school diploma. About 18 percent of them had received a college degree of some kind.

From the American take-over until 1914, English was the primary language in which public-school classes were conducted. Since 1915 all public schools conduct classes in Spanish. English is taught as a second language and is compulsory.

Puerto Rico has more than fifty colleges and universities. The oldest and biggest public university system is the University of Puerto Rico, which has eleven

Courses in technology are popular in Puerto Rican secondary schools and colleges.

campuses around the island. The largest private universities include Interamerican University and Caribbean University.

RELIGION

The Roman Catholic Church has a long and respected history in Puerto Rico. The first diocese, or church district, in the Americas was established in Puerto Rico in 1511 by the Spanish. While most Puerto Ricans are Roman Catholic, Protestant denominations have gained many members in recent decades, especially Pentecostalism, and may claim a third or more of the population.

Such traditional African religions as Santeria and Ifá, brought to the region by African slaves centuries ago, are still practiced by a few people. Puerto Rico is also home to the largest community of Jewish people in the Caribbean, numbering about three thousand. No other island in the Caribbean has representatives of the Conservative, Reform, and Orthodox branches of Judaism.

Catholic mass is celebrated in the Cathedral of Old San Juan, the second oldest cathedral in the Western Hemisphere.

AN AFRICAN FIESTA

In the seventeenth century a fisherman in Loíza found a small wooden statue of a knight on horseback hidden in a cork tree. He took the statue home, but the statue turned up missing. He went back to the cork tree, and there it was. The fisherman took the statue home again, and once again it disappeared. He returned to the tree and found it back in its hiding place. This time he took the statue to the local priest. The priest told him it was a statue of Santiago (St. James) and blessed it, which apparently was enough to keep the statue from popping back into its tree. Ever since then Loíza has held a saint's day festival in honor of Santiago.

This festival is different from other celebrations, however, because Loíza, a town near San Juan, is composed almost entirely of people of African descent. Forbidden from worshiping their own gods by the Spaniards, the Africans used the saint's day festival as an excuse to celebrate their god Shango, known as the god of thunder and lightning in the Yorùbá religion. Even today an African influence can be seen in some of the costumes worn by the revelers. Traditional costumes include coconut-headed devils called *vejiantes*, tattered old men called *viejos*, and Spanish knights called *caballeros*. The elaborate costumes have made Loíza's festival the most famous on the island.

SPORTS

One of the most popular sports in Puerto Rico is baseball. Such great Puerto Rican ballplayers as Roberto Clemente and Orlando Cepeda are heroes in both the United States and Puerto Rico. More recent Major League players of Puerto Rican descent include Edgar Mártinez, who retired from the Seattle Mariners in 2004, and David DeJesus, who currently plays for the Kansas City Royals.

Boxing is another popular sport. Puerto Rico was home to the third most boxers at the professional world champion level. Other popular sports include volleyball and basketball. The Puerto Rican national basketball team has participated in nine Olympic Games since 1960. In the 2004 Games in Athens, Greece, it became the first team to

The Puerto Rican national baseball team is currently the tenth ranked baseball team in the world.

defeat a U.S. team made up of National Basketball Association players. The world champion Puerto Rican All-Stars play basketball while riding unicycles!

ART AND LITERATURE

Puerto Ricans are proud of their artists and writers. The Institute of Puerto Rican Culture helps promote the work of native artists, writers, musicians, and other performing artists. One of the most admired Puerto Rican artists was Rafael Tufiño, known as the "Painter of the People." He painted ordinary people and beautiful landscapes of his homeland. Tufiño believed "that art should be accessible, that it should be for the people." He was born in New York City but moved to San Juan with his grandmother when he was ten years old. Tufiño divided much of his later years between New York and Puerto Rico. When Rafael Tufiño died at the age of eighty-five in 2008, the governor of Puerto Rico declared two days of national mourning.

Puerto Rican literature is rich in poetry, stories, and novels. Among the best-known Puerto Rican authors is Pedro Juan Soto, who lived for a time in the United States and wrote a book of short stories about the struggles of Puerto Ricans who immigrated to New York City. Olga Nolla, who died in 2001, was a poet, writer, and teacher. She spoke out in her writing for women's rights and edited a magazine that featured women writers. Francisco Arrivi, who died in 2007, is one of the island's greatest playwrights and is known as "The Father of the Puerto Rican Theater." He helped launch theater festivals across Puerto Rico. A leading contemporary writer, Zoé Jiménez Corretjer, has written twelve books and teaches literature at the University of Puerto Rico in Humaco. Her nonfiction book *La Mano Que Escribe* (The Hand That Writes) won the First National Essay Award given by the Pen Club of Puerto Rico in 2008.

POPULATION DENSITY

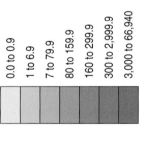

Persons per square mile

| 0.0 to 0.9 | 1 to 6.9 | 7 to 79.9 | 80 to 159.9 | 160 to 299.9 | 300 to 2,999.9 | 3,000 to 66,940 |

A DIFFERENT TEMPO

The image of Puerto Rico as a tropical island where people tend to take life easy is largely true. With the year-round warm climate comes a more relaxed way of life. Though this jam-packed island is no longer a wild, tropical paradise, some places still have a sleepy feel. "You're in the tropics now," one Puerto Rican explained, "and you have to learn to slow down. Take some time to enjoy the scenery."

"Coming from the States, it takes some time to adjust," says one frequent traveler. "Over there, everything is produce, produce, produce. Here you have to slow down. It's a different tempo."

People enjoy their leisure time in Puerto Rico, as does this father flying kites with his daughter in San Juan.

THE HAPPIEST PEOPLE IN THE WORLD

Puerto Ricans have always known that they are happy and content. Now the whole world knows it, too. In 2005 the World Values Survey, the largest social science study ever, announced the results of its evaluation of eighty-two societies for their state of well-being. Puerto Rico ranked number one in the survey, which was based on interviews with 120,000 people around the world. The United States came in fifteenth place.

Contributing factors to Puerto Ricans' happiness, according to the survey, include warmth to each other and strangers, a strong focus on the family, and a love of celebrating special events and occasions. The results did not surprise retired government worker Enrique Rodríguez. "We are a small island, and people are nice to each other," he says. "Everybody gets along. When we pass in the street, we say hello to each other."

Radio and TV show host Lily Garcia sees it more philosophically. "The Latin temperament is to be very optimistic in many ways," says Garcia. "We just kind of make the best out of it, out of everything. That's an important part of being happy."

Of course, there is a big difference between life in the San Juan area and traditional life in the country, or *campo*. One woman who lives just outside San Juan says, "If I go to New York, it's *too* crowded. There's too much noise. Here it's calm." But when she visits her relatives in the campo, it's too quiet. "I can't go for too long to a place that's so quiet. I like to see people, hear noises, and see people arguing. At my mother's, all you see is some chickens around, and some pigs. A week is good, but to live there, I wouldn't like it."

Life is less peaceful in the crowded streets of the San Juan metropolitan area and other cities and large towns. Driving, for example, can be anything but relaxing. Waiting for a gap to open in the traffic is hopeless; you just have to plunge in. Longtime resident Susie Fairbank jokes, "Everyone drives really well, because everyone is such a bad driver, you have to drive really well not to get hit." Baseball star Sandy Alomar Jr. put it more bluntly: "Driving in Puerto Rico is crazy. If you don't drive crazy, they kill you."

Some city dwellers escape the stress by fleeing town on the weekends. No matter where you live in Puerto Rico, you are never far from a beach. "When you are there you feel free to do whatever you want," says sixth-grader Aura Alonso. "You always hear the music of the water." Sixth-grader Litza Acosta says, "I like to find shells and see starfishes. But the thing that I love the most is having time with my family at the beach."

MONUMENTO DE LA RECORDACION · MEMORIAL MONUMENT

Chapter Four

Working It Out

Puerto Rico is neither a state of the United States nor a country, but something in between—a commonwealth. It is considered an "associated free state" linked to the United States, but it is not free to end this association unless the U.S. Congress agrees.

Puerto Rico's government is similar to that of a U.S. state. Puerto Ricans elect a legislature that passes laws governing the island, but the U.S. government retains many important powers. The Puerto Rican government runs the schools, roads, and police, while U.S. laws regulate the environment, labor rules, and trade with other countries.

Puerto Ricans are U.S. citizens, but they do not vote in U.S. presidential elections or pay federal taxes, unless they move to a U.S. state. Puerto Ricans have, however, been drafted to fight in every U.S. war since World War I. The U.S. government pays for many programs in Puerto Rico, but Puerto Ricans have no senators or representatives in the U.S. Congress— just one nonvoting delegate.

The Capitol in San Juan was completed in 1929. The commonwealth's constitution is exhibited in its central rotunda.

INSIDE GOVERNMENT

Like the United States, Puerto Rico has three branches of government: executive, legislative, and judicial.

Executive

The head of the executive branch is the governor, who is elected to a four-year term. The governor appoints many important officials, including a council of secretaries who run various departments. The governor can prevent bills passed by the legislature from becoming law by vetoing them. But if two-thirds of both the house and the senate vote for the bill again, it becomes a law. In 2000 Puerto Ricans elected their first female governor, Sila Maria Calderón, a former mayor of San Juan.

Sila Maria Calderón, seventh governor of the Commonwealth of Puerto Rico from 2001 to 2005, is the first woman elected to that office.

In 2008 Luis G. Fortuño, a lawyer and Puerto Rico's nonvoting representative in the U.S. Congress, was elected governor by one of the widest margins in decades. Fortuño wants to reduce the size of the commonwealth's government to save money and help a slumping economy. "My message all along was that we had to pull together, that we had lost hope, our ability to dream," he said soon after his election. "It is the only way to go."

Legislative

The legislative branch consists of a senate and a house of representatives, whose members propose and vote on the laws of Puerto Rico. Senators and representatives are elected to four-year terms. The house of representatives includes one member from each of forty districts, plus eleven representatives-at-large, who represent the entire island instead of one district. The senate has two members from each of eight districts, plus eleven senators-at-large. If one party controls more than two-thirds of either house, however, more members are selected until other parties have at least one-third of the total.

Judicial

The judicial branch is headed by judges, who decide how to apply the law to settle disputes. Most cases involving serious crimes are tried in the superior court. The supreme court's seven justices are appointed by the governor and approved by the senate. They serve until age seventy. If someone disagrees with a ruling in the superior court, the person can ask the court of appeals to review the case. If appealed again, Puerto Rico's supreme court

Puerto Rican governor Luis Fortuño (left), ninth and current governor of the Commonwealth of Puerto Rico, welcomes congress members in San Juan.

makes a final judgment. The governor also appoints judges to the superior court and the circuit court of appeals. There is also a court system on the island for trying federal cases.

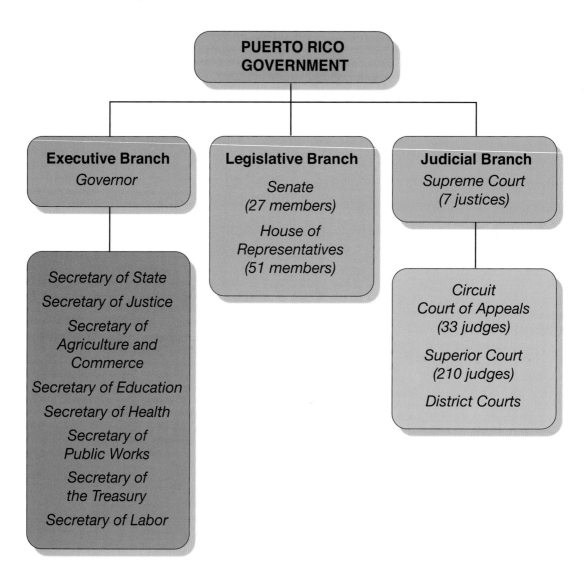

PUERTO RICO GOVERNMENT

Executive Branch
Governor

Secretary of State

Secretary of Justice

Secretary of Agriculture and Commerce

Secretary of Education

Secretary of Health

Secretary of Public Works

Secretary of the Treasury

Secretary of Labor

Legislative Branch
Senate (27 members)

House of Representatives (51 members)

Judicial Branch
Supreme Court (7 justices)

Circuit Court of Appeals (33 judges)

Superior Court (210 judges)

District Courts

DOÑA FELA

One of Puerto Rico's most popular politicians, Felisa Rincón de Gautier, had a career that spanned the twentieth century. Born in Ceiba in 1897, she entered politics by helping Puerto Rican women win the right to vote in 1932. She then helped Luis Muñoz Marín create the PPD in 1938. Eight years later she was elected mayor of San Juan, a job she held for twenty-two years. As mayor she set up a system that allowed her to have direct contact with every neighborhood in San Juan, which kept her informed about the needs of the city's poorest citizens. She helped launch the Head Start program in San Juan, which provides poor children with a preschool education. Her program was so successful that it served as a model for the U.S. Head Start program on the mainland.

Doña Fela, as she was popularly known, was beloved by many Puerto Ricans. She once sent an airplane full of snow to Puerto Rico, because the island's children had never seen snow before. Doña Fela died in 1994 at the age of ninety-seven.

THE STATUS QUESTION

The issue that has dominated political debate ever since the U.S. invasion in 1898 is what form of government Puerto Rico should have. Specifically, people argue about how closely Puerto Rico should be tied to the United States. Staying a commonwealth, writer Esmeralda Santiago contends, is a way to hide from "the question of what we are as a people. . . . It is not a choice. It is a refusal to choose."

Gaining statehood would give Puerto Rico representation in the U.S. Congress. But it would also force individuals and businesses to pay U.S. taxes. "Statehood?" scoffs one resident. "The fat cats would never let it happen. They don't want the taxman down here." And many people worry that if Puerto Rico were absorbed into the United States, it might lose its unique culture.

Puerto Ricans in favor of independence argue that ties to the United States harm Puerto Rico by making it dependent on outside aid. U.S. government spending helps provide Puerto Ricans with roads, schools, housing, food, and health care. More than half of Puerto Rico's residents receive food stamps. One North American who moved to Puerto Rico believes U.S. government handouts have eroded people's work ethic and self-respect. "It's our fault," he says. "We did it to them. You give a man food and a place to live without working, and you destroy him."

For many Puerto Ricans the desire for independence is outweighed by the knowledge that most of their neighbors in the Caribbean are even poorer. They don't like being dependent on outsiders, but the alternative seems worse. Independence would mean losing U.S. citizenship, and with it the right to live and work in the United States.

PUERTO RICO
BY COUNTY

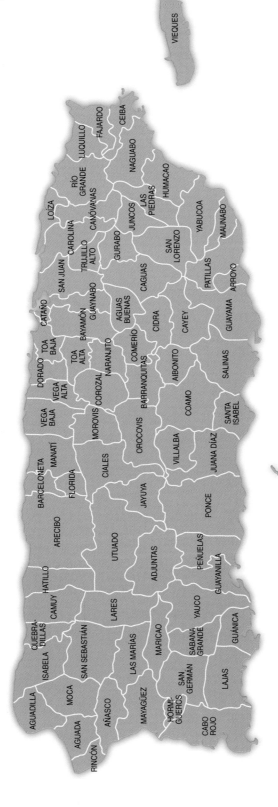

A SHORTAGE OF TEACHERS

One of the biggest problems facing the educational system in Puerto Rico today is the loss of teachers to the mainland. As more and more Hispanics have moved to the United States from Latin America, the demand for bilingual teachers who can teach in Spanish and English has grown enormously, especially in states with high Hispanic populations like California. Educational officials from these states have lured hundreds of Puerto Rican teachers north over the past decade with high wages and free graduate school programs. As recently as 2008, school officials from New Haven, Connecticut, recruited eight Puerto Rican teachers to come to their state to work.

The teacher shortage has hurt Puerto Rican schools at a time when administrators are trying to promote the teaching of English in schools. In public schools classes are conducted in Spanish and students aren't exposed to English until high school. In private schools, however, all classes, except for Spanish, are conducted in English.

"I personally doubt that Puerto Rico will ever be independent," says Marta Ramos, an officer at Puerto Rico's largest bank. "We're too Americanized, too used to American ways—cars, jobs, U.S. money. We're economically dependent. All the road money comes from the Department of Transportation. All the social programs, all the money comes from the U.S. To call all that off and try to start on your own—it's not going

Children wave flags of Puerto Rico and the United States during a Fourth of July celebration, expressing their dual loyalties.

to happen. We don't have the resources. We have beautiful beaches, but that's not going to support an economy."

So the debate continues. In recent years a growing number of voters has supported closer ties with the mainland. In 1993, 49 percent of Puerto Rican voters supported commonwealth status, while 46 percent supported statehood and 4 percent supported independence. In 1998, 47 percent supported statehood, while 50 percent rejected statehood, the commonwealth, and independence. They voted instead for "none of the above," indicating that while many are frustrated with the present arrangement, they don't see an easy way to improve it. Governor Fortuño favors statehood but sees serious economic problems made worse by a recent recession as a higher priority at present. It is unlikely that the controversy over the status of Puerto Rico will be settled anytime soon.

Chapter Five

Making a Living

Making a living in Puerto Rico has always been difficult. In the 1990s it got even harder, when the tax breaks that U.S. businesses received for locating there were reduced. Most were phased out entirely by 2006, making Puerto Rico less desirable to U.S. businesses. Without the tax breaks, Puerto Rico has lost jobs to other countries where wages are lower. Businesses can hire workers in the Dominican Republic, a neighboring Caribbean country, for about one-tenth what they pay Puerto Ricans.

Although Puerto Rico has a strong university system, many people with college degrees have had to move to the mainland to get good jobs. "The kids that go to the university—when they come out, they can't find a job," says working mother Delia Morales. "A lot of kids end up working in fast food places." The unemployment rate in 2006 was nearly 12 percent, almost two and a half times the average in the United States at that time.

AGRICULTURE AND NATURAL RESOURCES

Agriculture, once the main industry on the island, now employs just 1.3 percent of the workforce. Coffee is the island's most valuable crop.

Sugarcane, once the principle crop of Puerto Rico, is being cut down by a worker with a machete.

Fruits such as bananas, mangoes, coconuts, and pineapples are also major crops. Farmers raise chickens and cows, while fish and lobster are harvested from the sea.

Puerto Rico is the world's largest producer of rum, a liquor made from molasses, which comes from sugarcane. Sugarcane, once raised on vast plantations, is still grown on the island but in far smaller quantities than in the past. Today, Puerto Rico must import molasses from the Dominican Republic to keep its rum factories in operation.

Today sugarcane is grown and raised in small quantities in Puerto Rico.

COFFEE—A FAMILY BUSINESS

For a century the Atienza family has grown some of the finest coffee beans (below) in the world on its 340-acre plantation in Jayuya, Puerto Rico. However, it looked like the family business might come to an end as the coffee market declined over several decades. Recently, the renewed popularity of gourmet coffee in the United States and elsewhere has revitalized the market. Roberto Atienza, grandson of the plantation's founder, has added gourmet coffee to his crop and finds it highly profitable.

Every step of the coffee-making process is handled with great care. When the fruit of the coffee bushes ripen, pickers pick it and remove the pulp to expose the seeds inside. The seeds, or beans, are washed and dried by machines. Atienza, like his grandfather before him, sleeps on a cot next to the machine so he can arise regularly to check that the beans are drying properly. The beans are then roasted and packaged to be sent to the United States and elsewhere.

But there is one problem facing Atienza and other coffee growers on the island—a shortage of workers. Most young people would rather work in the service industry than do the hard work of harvesting coffee beans. "My average coffee picker is between fifty and sixty years old," says Atienza." In ten more years, there will probably be no pickers left." To entice workers, Atienza has offered them free transportation to the coffee fields, meals with music, and even raffle prizes. "We have to provide incentives, or else no one would come," he says. The government has used prison labor to help with the harvest and has considered starting short-term foreign guest-worker programs.

PUERTO RICO WORKFORCE

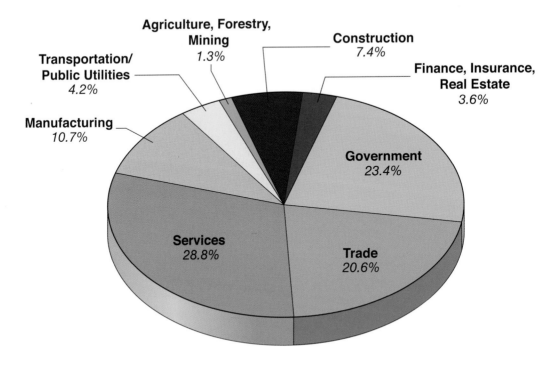

Agriculture, Forestry, Mining
1.3%

Construction
7.4%

Transportation/Public Utilities
4.2%

Finance, Insurance, Real Estate
3.6%

Manufacturing
10.7%

Government
23.4%

Services
28.8%

Trade
20.6%

Stone, sand, and gravel are mined on the island. Political battles rage from time to time over whether mining companies should be allowed to dig up the valuable stores of copper and nickel in the central mountains, which would spoil their beauty. Puerto Rico's scenery is an important attraction for tourists.

TOURISM

Tourism is a multibillion-dollar industry in Puerto Rico. In 2007 the island was visited by nearly 6 million tourists, many of them from the United States. More than 10 million passengers fly into Luis Muñoz

Marín International Airport near San Juan, making it the busiest airport in the Caribbean. Some leave from there for other Caribbean destinations. Cruise ships docking in the port of San Juan bring more tourists for short stays.

Cruise ships are a common sight in San Juan's harbors.

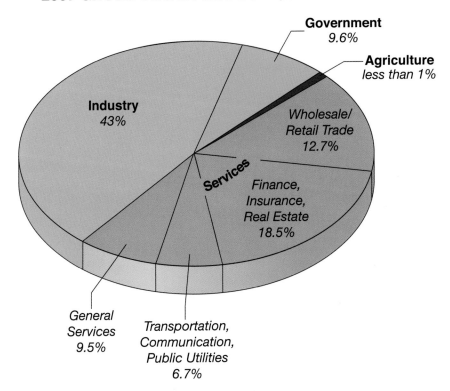

2007 GROSS STATE PRODUCT: $90 Million

Government
9.6%

Agriculture
less than 1%

Industry
43%

Wholesale/
Retail Trade
12.7%

Services

Finance,
Insurance,
Real Estate
18.5%

General
Services
9.5%

Transportation,
Communication,
Public Utilities
6.7%

According to the World Travel and Tourism Council, travel and tourism accounted for 5.7 percent of the gross domestic product of Puerto Rico in 2009 and provided 73,000 jobs in the workforce. This accounts for about one in every eighteen jobs on the island. Out of twenty-three countries in the Caribbean, Puerto Rico ranked second in the size of its tourism industry in 2009, and sixty-eighth in the world.

INDUSTRY AND TECHNOLOGY

Since the late 1940s industry has surpassed agriculture in importance in the Puerto Rican economy. Manufacturing accounts for 10.7 percent of all jobs on the island. More than one hundred drug companies have plants in Puerto Rico. Pharmaceuticals, electronics, medical equipment, and apparel are among the biggest manufactured exports.

In 2006 ground was broken for the Bioprocess Training and Development Complex in Mayagüez, near the University of Puerto Rico campus. The complex is a joint venture between Puerto Rican private businesses and the U.S. Economic Development Administration. "By strengthening ties between government, industry, and academia, we remain competitive in a global economy and provide good, private sector jobs for Puerto Ricans," said then-governor Anibal Acevedo Vilá.

The pharmaceutical sector in Puerto Rico employs approximately 28,000 people.

EARNING A LIVING

ATLANTIC OCEAN

Caribbean Sea

Mona Island

Culebra Island

Vieques Island

San Juan

Aguadilla
Aguada
Isabela
Camuy
San Sebastián
Lares
Añasco
Mayagüez
San Germán
Yauco
Adjuntas
Utuado
Arecibo
Manatí
Toa Baja
Bayamón
Barranquitas
Ponce
Guayama
Cayey
Caguas
Guaynabo
Carolina
Trujillo Alto
Humacao
Yabucoa
Guayama
Fajardo
Ceiba

Lago de Guajataca
Río Culebrinas
Río Grande de Añasco
Río Yauco
Lago de Patillas
Río Grande de Arecibo
Lago Dos Bocas
Río Grande de Manatí
Río de Bayamón
Río La Plata
Cibuco
Río de

Agriculture

Bananas

Beef cattle

Coconuts

Coffee

Natural Resources

Lime

Salt

Sand and gravel

Manufacturing

Pharmaceuticals

Textiles

Lobster

Milk

Pineapple

Poultry

Sugar

Tobacco

Tuna

ECONOMIC PROBLEMS

Despite these positive signs the Puerto Rican economy is facing many challenges in the twenty-first century. A recession that began in 2005 led to a $3.2 billion budget deficit by 2009. On May 1, 2006, the government took the unprecedented step of shutting down forty-three government agencies to reduce spending and imposed a new sales tax. Among the closed agencies was the Department of Education, which shut down all 1,536 public schools.

The closings were temporary and did not solve the commonwealth's cash flow problems. In March 2009 Governor Fortuño announced that starting in July of that year, he would have to lay off 30,000 out of a total of 130,000 government employees, and freeze government salaries for two years. He said the cumulative deficit by the end of the fiscal year could reach $21 billion. Fortuño planned to borrow $1.2 billion from state banks in 2009. The money will be used to pay old debts and fund an economic stimulus package.

Chapter Six

A Tropical Tour

Tourists who go to Puerto Rico and spend their whole vacation on the beach in front of their hotel are missing a lot. To see what's special about Puerto Rico, you've got to get out and about. Puerto Rico is a small island, so you're never more than a few hours' drive from anything.

SAN JUAN

The city of San Juan is one of the oldest capital cities in the Western Hemisphere and is filled with historic sites. A favorite is El Morro, the huge stone fort on a point of land projecting into San Juan Harbor. Exhibits there describe the fort's long history, including its role in clashes with pirates and Dutch, English, and American invaders. El Morro's tower, which is still standing, was built in 1539. Shell fragments fired by U.S. troops during the Spanish-American War in 1898 are still lodged in the fort's wall. El Morro's many levels and circular and triangular staircases make it feel like a giant maze, and it is a great place to explore.

El Yunque is an excellent choice for a rainforest experience with its overwhelming beauty.

LA ROGATIVA

In 1797 Great Britain sent about sixty ships and approximately nine thousand men to capture Puerto Rico from Spain. English troops surrounded San Juan for two weeks. The people of San Juan grew sick and hungry as they waited for Spanish soldiers to rescue them.

According to legend the English siege failed when Puerto Rican women sang hymns for divine intercession called a *rogativa* to Saint Ursula and Saint Catherine. At the darkest moment of the siege the Spanish governor called for all the women of San Juan to march through the town. The women, led by the bishop, carried torches, and the streets rang with bells. Hearing the noise and seeing the march by torchlight, the English soldiers thought Spanish troops had arrived, and they fled.

Today a statue called *La Rogativa* (below) stands on a hill overlooking San Juan Harbor. The dramatic statue shows the women of San Juan marching through the streets to save their city.

An old stone wall hugs the coastline to another fort, San Cristóbal, which protected the city from land invasions. Behind the huge wall between these forts is historic Old San Juan. This seven-square-block area is filled with churches and museums that showcase the city's history, music, and art. A stroll down almost any narrow street reveals beautiful old houses painted pale lavender, pink, green, orange, or brown. Metal bars called *rejas* (RAH-hahs) crisscross the windows in lovely patterns, serving as both decorative art and protection. Though there are plenty of bustling shops and restaurants, a stroll at twilight down the quiet side streets is

This three-story apartment building in Old San Juan has been restored to its original elegance.

magical. Some of these streets are so narrow, you can touch the two side walls simply by stretching out your arms.

Old San Juan, however, is just a tiny corner of a modern, bustling metropolis. The Río Piedras Market offers rows of stalls that sell fruits, vegetables, and clothes. There are dozens of modern hotels right on the beach. The Puerto Rico Convention Center, completed in 2005, is the largest and most technically advanced building of its kind in the Caribbean. It can accommodate ten thousand people.

But San Juan is just the start of our island tour. To see Puerto Rico in all its splendor, you must go, as the natives say, "out on the island."

HEAD FOR THE HILLS

Sun and sand may represent Puerto Rico in travel posters, but the island's mountains are just as spectacular. The bigger cities and the beaches are arranged in a ring around the coast. Leaving this loop to go inland inevitably means going up, up, and up. Narrow, winding roads zigzag up the hillsides. You'll often gasp as cars hurtle toward you around tight curves. Roadside stands selling fruit and barbecued meat dot a scenic road called the Ruta Panorámica. Around every turn, some lucky family has a house with a dazzling view nestled in the hills.

The mountains of the Cordillera Central are incredibly lush. In some places the hills seem to foam with vegetation. And if you ascend to the top of any peak, you can usually find a town. One of the most beautiful towns with a very hilly terrain is San Germán, settled in 1511, the second-oldest Spanish settlement in Puerto Rico. San Germán is famous for an austere chapel named Porta Coeli, "the Gates of Heaven," which dates from 1606. The church's ceiling still contains the original beams, made of nearly indestructible ausubo wood. The town also boasts gorgeous central plazas and awesome views from houses hugging the steep hillsides.

Another historic mountain town is Lares, the site of the 1868 uprising known as El Grito de Lares. You can read about the proud history of the independence movement on the walls of the local ice cream parlor, Heladería Lares, which opened in 1968, on the one hundredth anniversary of the uprising. The store's offerings include an array of ice cream flavors based on local foods, like avocado, corn, beans, rice, tomatoes, carrots, celery, sugarcane, ginger, and green bean. Be daring—you can taste before you buy.

The Ruta Panorámica, or Panoramic Route, winds its way through the mountains of the Cordillera Central in the heart of Puerto Rico for about 100 miles. This is the most scenic drive in the Caribbean.

PLACES TO SEE

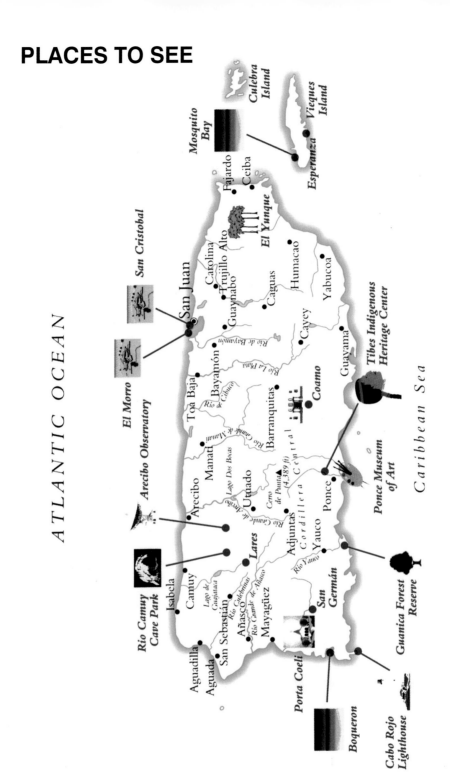

ATLANTIC OCEAN

Mosquito Bay

Culebra Island

Vieques Island

Esperanza

San Cristobal

San Juan

El Morro

Fajardo

Ceiba

El Yunque

Carolina

Trujillo Alto

Guaynabo

Caguas

Humacao

Yabucoa

Arecibo Observatory

Río de Bayamón

Cavey

Guayama

Tibes Indigenous Heritage Center

Toa Baja

Bayamón

Río de Cibuco

Río La Plata

Coamo

Caribbean Sea

Manatí

Río Grande de Manatí

Barranquitas

Lago Dos Bocas

Utuado

Río Grande de Arecibo

Cerro de Punta (4,389 ft)

Cordillera Central

Ponce Museum of Art

Arecibo

Adjuntas

Yauco

Ponce

Rio Camuy Cave Park

Lares

Río Yauco

Guánica Forest Reserve

Isabela

Camuy

Lago de Guajataca

Río Culebrinas

San Germán

Aguadilla

Aguada

San Sebastián

Añasco

Río Grande de Añasco

Mayagüez

Porta Coeli

Boqueron

Cabo Rojo Lighthouse

Mona Island

KARST AND CAVES

The northwest part of the island is karst country, filled with lumpy, improbable shapes created when underground limestone caves collapsed to create pits on the surface called sinkholes. Scientists took advantage of one of these deep circular pits to build a giant radio-antenna dish for the Arecibo Observatory in 1963. This vast bowl, 1,000 feet wide and lined with 40,000 aluminum mirrors, focuses radio waves from outer space onto a platform suspended 450 feet in the air. It is the largest radio telescope in the world, and its location near the equator allows it to scan the skies of both the Northern and Southern hemispheres, listening for signals from the far reaches of the universe. Scientists at Arecibo have made some amazing discoveries, including finding the first planets outside our solar system.

Located in Puerto Rico, the Arecibo Observatory is the largest radio telescope on Earth.

Tourists gaze at the Espiral Sinkhole cave at Río Camuy Cave Park, a 268-acre park that is the site of the great subterranean caverns carved out by the Camuy River over a million years ago.

The telescope is also used to listen for signs of intelligent life in other parts of the universe. The observatory was featured in the movie *Contact*, in which Jodie Foster played a scientist who received messages from aliens. Even if you're not interested in science, you'll enjoy the drive through the surrounding karst country, with its unearthly landscapes.

Not too far from the observatory is the Río Camuy Cave Park. The underground rivers that dissolved the limestone to make sinkholes also carved miles of underground caves, creating one of the largest underground river systems in the world. Tour guides lead visitors through an awe-inspiring underground chamber 200 feet wide and 170 feet high. You can peer down 150 feet at the ancient river that began carving the cave more than a million years ago. Rippled ribbons of rock called draperies decorate the walls, and hanging formations called stalactites cling to the ceilings. So many bats live in Río Camuy Cave that when the people making the movie *Batman Forever* needed bat sounds for their soundtrack, they came to these echoing caverns to record them.

BACK TO THE BEACH

Descending the mountains to the western coast, you'll find some of Puerto Rico's most inviting beaches. In the northwestern corner steep red cliffs drop right to the water. You'll also find beaches with high winds and waves that make them popular spots for surfers.

At the southwestern corner of the island is the famous swimming beach of Boquerón. Rows of palm trees, neatly mowed grass, and a vast expanse of white sand make it an ideal place for sunning and swimming. You won't find aquatic plants or coral at Boquerón, just the calm water and soft sand that Puerto Ricans consider the perfect beach.

Boquerón Beach, situated in southeast Puerto Rico, is over a mile long and borders sparkling turquoise waters.

Barely 20 miles away, at the island's southwest corner, are Puerto Rico's steepest cliffs, rising above the Caribbean Sea. At the Cabo Rojo Lighthouse you can walk out on a narrow ridge that drops straight down on both sides for hundreds of feet. At this windswept point you feel like you are at the end of the world. The bumpy dirt road leading to the lighthouse is nearly impassable after a rain, but the slow trip is made

Cabo Rojo Lighthouse, the third lighthouse built in Puerto Rico, is considered to have some of the most spectacular ocean views in Puerto Rico's West Coast.

Waves lap up on a rocky beach at the Guánica Dry Forest Reserve in the island's arid southwest.

enchanting by the many crabs that scuttle along the road, holding their claws in the air. The nearby Cabo Rojo Salt Flats is a national wildlife refuge and a favorite nesting place for migratory shorebirds.

The southwest is the island's dry side. At the Guánica Dry Forest Reserve you can see the strange sight of cactuses growing right next to the beach. It's the wildest, most exotic place on the island. Where a dirt road ends, you can walk into the reserve along the rocky shore, feeling the bubbles of volcanic rock crunch beneath your feet. You won't find the smooth, white sand of the more popular beaches here, but you can wade into the water and see plants, rocks, and countless tropical fish in a variety of stripes and colors. It's like climbing into an aquarium. Just across the road the harsh landscape is filled with flowering cactuses and spiny, poisonous plants. Farther inland, trails lead through a forest that houses more species of birds than any other place on the island.

This antique Ford fire engine is one of the treasures of Ponce's Parque de Bombas, a museum dedicated to firefighting history.

In the middle of the southern coast is the city of Ponce, known as La Perla del Sur, or "the Pearl of the South." Though Ponce is Puerto Rico's fourth-largest city, it feels very different from modern, urban San Juan. Founded in 1692 by Juan Ponce de León's great-grandson Loíza Ponce de León, Ponce is centered on a lovely square filled with trees and fountains. Surrounding the square is a historic district with handsome buildings. The town hall is open and welcoming, with airy courtyards and hallways lined with paintings made by leading artists. Right on the square is perhaps the brightest building in Puerto Rico, the red-and-black-striped Parque de Bombas, a former fire station, now a museum. Decorated with curlicues and firefighting memorabilia, it looks more like a children's playhouse than a museum. You should also stop by the grand Ponce Museum of Art. The museum was designed by Edward Durell Stone, who also designed New York City's Radio City Music Hall. The museum's collection, containing more than three thousand works of art, includes paintings by European masters and Puerto Rico's finest artists, including José Campeche and Francisco Oller y Cestero.

TEN LARGEST CITIES

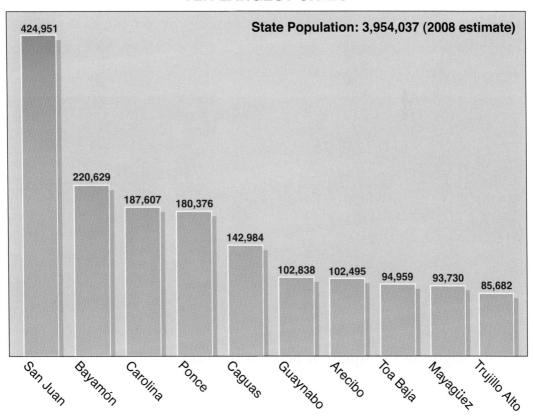

State Population: 3,954,037 (2008 estimate)

City	Population
San Juan	424,951
Bayamón	220,629
Carolina	187,607
Ponce	180,376
Caguas	142,984
Guaynabo	102,838
Arecibo	102,495
Toa Baja	94,959
Mayagüez	93,730
Trujillo Alto	85,682

A must for anyone interested in the island's American-Indian history is the Tibes Indigenous Ceremonial Center just outside of Ponce. This pre-Columbian site was discovered in 1975, when Hurricane Eloise flooded the city. When the waters receded, ancient artifacts were exposed. Tibes was the island's largest ceremonial meeting place for the Taíno people and their ancestors. Ten ball courts, or *bateyes*, have been reconstructed, the biggest 111 by 118 feet. You can also enter reconstructed houses. A museum contains pottery and carved stone sculptures made by the island's early inhabitants. It also has displays about their food, clothing, and customs, such as inhaling the drug *cohaba*, which they believed let them talk with spirits and see the future. One visitor recognized the gourds the Indians used for bowls. They looked just like the one his grandfather had—he refused to eat from anything else.

A reconstructed Indian ball court twists around the landscape at the Tibes Indigenous Ceremonial Center near Ponce.

PONCE ON THE MARCH

The beauty of downtown Ponce stands as a shining example of what can be done with responsible government spending. In the 1980s the grand buildings of Ponce's historic zone were in ruins. Then in 1985 a Ponce resident, Rafael Hernández Colón became governor for a second term and shifted $600 million of government money to his neglected hometown. Under a program called Ponce on the March, hundreds of stately buildings were restored, utility wires were hidden from view, and the city reclaimed its title as Pearl of the South. The funding was yanked when a new governor was elected in 1993. More recently the urban renewal has restarted and once again the city of Ponce is on the march.

While heading northeast, stop in Coamo, Puerto Rico's third-oldest town. Coamo is in a valley, encircled by many hills that make it feel like a world of its own. Near Coamo are hot springs that residents have been enjoying for hundreds, if not thousands, of years. It is believed that Ponce de León was told by natives that the hot springs were the legendary Fountain of Youth. He mistakenly thought the magical fountain was in Florida, which he later explored. Coamo's hot springs now flow into two huge swimming pools that can accommodate entire families of health-seekers.

From the eastern tip of the island you can catch a ferry to the island of Vieques. It's a beautiful ride, and you pass by several smaller islands, called keys, on the way. After the crowds and traffic of the big island, Vieques looks like a real tropical paradise. In May 2003 the controversial U.S. missile range on Vieques closed, and the American government turned over the military base to the Puerto Rican government.

In the tourist town of Esperanza you can snorkel right under the town pier and see lots of fish or swim ten minutes out to a smaller key surrounded by plants, fish, and coral. Esperanza is about the only town in Puerto Rico without a traffic jam. But on Saturday nights there is a people jam when everyone comes out to stroll back and forth on the main street by the beach.

This peaceful agave pasture in Vieques heralds a new day for this island, once the site of a U.S. missile range.

TINY SHOOTING STARS

The most magical place in Puerto Rico is Mosquito Bay on the island of Vieques. The bay's waters actually glow in the dark. They are filled with billions of tiny creatures called dinoflagellates that produce a burst of light when jostled. If your boat startles a group of these creatures, you'll see streaks of light in the water as they dart away. If you jump in for a swim, each movement will leave a glowing trail. Cup the water in your hands, and it sparkles like fairy dust. "People often tell me this is the most incredible thing they've ever seen," says one tour guide.

Mosquito Bay connects to the ocean by a single narrow channel. This keeps the glowing creatures penned in like fireflies in a bottle. Each gallon of water in Mosquito Bay contains 720,000 dinoflagellates. There were once many more places like this in the world, but only a handful are left. Some were destroyed by widening the channel, causing the dinoflagellates to flow out to sea. A similar bay near La Parguera on the main island was once as dazzling as Mosquito Bay. Because of pollution it is now only a tenth as bright as it once was.

To keep Mosquito Bay alive, tour guides don't use polluting gas powerboats but electric boats or kayaks.

The clear, rocky cove at Bahia des Tortuga on Culebra Island is a favorite among snorkelers.

If Vieques isn't quiet enough for you, visit the more rustic island of Culebra to the north. Much of it has been set aside as a wildlife refuge. It's as close to pure nature as you'll get, with great beaches and snorkeling.

A WALK IN THE RAIN FOREST

Our island tour has brought us full circle back to San Juan and one of the most beautiful sights in Puerto Rico, El Yunque rain forest. It is less than an hour's drive from the city. The forest is named for a 3,533-foot mountain peak in the Luquillo Mountains. El Yunque is the only tropical forest in the U.S. National Forest Service. The Luquillo Mountains catch the clouds sweeping in from the northeast, bringing rain to El Yunque nearly every day. That adds up to more than 100 billion gallons of rain a year.

This is the greenest place on a very green island. It's so wet that some plants have "drip tip" leaves, with little spouts that channel of water so they won't rot or grow fungus. Plants grow on top of plants—orchids grow on tree trunks, with vines draped over the lot. It feels like a fairy-tale jungle filled with the songs of coquís.

The greatest pleasure at El Yunque is watching the clouds float toward the mountain, no matter how sunny it is. If you're near the top of El Yunque, the clouds will appear to be coming straight toward you. Tendrils of mist collect against the hillside, and suddenly you're enveloped in fog. The fog thickens until you can't see a thing. Then comes the rain. In five minutes you're drenched. At times like this you can stumble along a trail to a scenic lookout point, unable to see 10 feet in front of you. But if you wait for the clouds to pass, the air slowly clears. Suddenly you can see the whole valley and the ocean in the distance. It's magnificent.

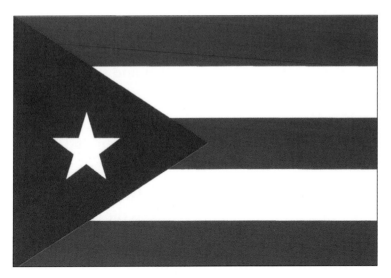

THE FLAG: *The Puerto Rico flag consists of three red and two white horizontal stripes, with a dark blue triangle against the left side. Inside the triangle is a white five-pointed star. The flag was adopted in 1952.*

THE SEAL: *A lamb in the center of the Puerto Rico seal symbolizes peace and brotherhood. Above the lamb are the letters F and I, which stand for Ferdinand and Isabella, the Spanish king and queen who were in power when Columbus arrived at Puerto Rico.*

Commonwealth Survey

Status: Puerto Rico became a commonwealth on July 25, 1952

Origin of Name: *Puerto Rico* is Spanish for "rich port"

Nickname: Isle of Enchantment

Capital: San Juan

Motto: John Is His Name

Bird: Stripe-headed tanager (*reinita mora*)

Animal: Coquí

Flower: Puerto Rican hibiscus (*flor de maga*)

Tree: Silk-cotton tree (ceiba)

Stripe-headed tanager

Puerto Rican hibiscus

LA BORINQUEÑA

Borinquen was the original Taíno name for the island that the Spaniards later renamed Puerto Rico. The song "La Borinqueña" is the official anthem of Puerto Rico.

La___ tier - ra de ¡Bo - rin - quen! Don - de he na - ci - do
Oh,___ my land of Bo - rin - quen! The land where I was

yo,___ Es___ un jar - dín flo - ri - do,
born,___ Gar - den so full of flow - ers,

de má - gi - co pri - mor'. Un cie - lo siem - pre ní - ti - do,
ma - gic - 'ly won - der - ful. Her sky for - ev - er lu - mi - nous,

la sir - ve de do - sel, Y dan ar - ru - llos plá - ci - dos
is like a can - o - py, And the waves gen - tle lull - a - by

las o - las a sus pies. Cuan - do a sus pla - ya lle - gó Co -
is a soft mel - o - dy. And when to this land Co - lum - bus

GEOGRAPHY

Highest Point: 4,389 feet above sea level, at Cerro de Punta

Lowest Point: Sea level, on the coast

Area: 3,515 square miles, including Culebra, Mona, and Vieques islands

Greatest Distance North to South: 40 miles

Greatest Distance East to West: about 110 miles

Hottest Recorded Temperature: 103 °F at San Lorenzo on
August 22, 1906

Coldest Recorded Temperature: 39 °F at Aibonito on March 9, 1911

Average Annual Precipitation: 70 inches in the north, 30 inches in
the south

Major Rivers: Añasco, Arecibo, Bayamón, Culebrinas, La Plata,
Loíza, Yauco

Major Lakes: Caonillas, Cartagena, Cidra, Guajataca, Loíza, San José

Trees: African tulip, ausubo, bay cedar, breadfruit, ceiba, coconut palm,
flamboyant, mahogany, mangrove, tabonuco, yagrumo hembra

Wild Plants: bunchgrass, cactus, damiana, guitarán, hibiscus, orchid,
poinsettia, rubber vine, tree fern

Animals: anole, bat, coquí, cucubano, firefly iguana, manatee, mongoose, snake

Birds: gorrión, red-tailed hawk, heron, hummingbird, nightingale, oriole, owl, gray kingbird, Puerto Rican bullfinch, thrasher

Fish: angelfish, barracuda, herring, marlin, mullet, pompano, shark, snapper, Spanish mackerel, tuna

Coquí

Endangered Animals: brown pelican, Caribbean monk seal, Culebra Island giant anole, finback whale, hawksbill sea turtle, leatherback sea turtle, Monito gecko, Puerto Rican boa, Puerto Rican broad-winged hawk, Puerto Rican nightjar, Puerto Rican parrot, Puerto Rican plain pigeon, Puerto Rican sharp-shinned hawk, sperm whale, Virgin Islands tree boa, West Indian manatee, yellow-shouldered blackbird

Endangered Plants: Puerto Rican maidenhair, Chase's threeawn, *Auerodendron pauciflorum*, bariaco, beautiful goetzea, *Calyptranthes thomasiana*, capa rosa, *Catesbaea melanocarpa*, Jamaican broom, chupacallos, Cook's holly, serpentine manjack, helmet orchid, *Daphnopsis hellerana*, Cerro de Punta jayuya, elfin tree fern, erubia, Woodbury's stopper, higuero de sierra, Sintenis' holly, babyboot orchid, sebucan, *Lyonia Proctor's staggerbush*, Maxwell's girdlepod, Cana Gorda girdlepod, ausu palo colorado, palo de jazmin, palo de nigua, palo de ramon, palo de rosa, pelos del diablo, Monte Guilarte hollyfern, St. Thomas prickly-ash, *Tectaria estremerana*, El Yunque Colorado, cordillera maiden fern, Barrio Charcas maiden fern, Puerto Rican maiden fern, uvillo, Vahl's boxwood, Proctor's veronica, West Indian walnut, Wheeler's peperonia

TIMELINE

Puerto Rico History

c. 2000 BCE Indians first arrive in Puerto Rico.

c. 400 BCE Ancestors of the Taíno come to Puerto Rico from South America.

1400s Taíno Indians live in small villages around the island, raising crops and fishing.

1508 Spaniard Juan Ponce de León founds Caparra, the first European settlement on the island.

1511 The Taíno rebel against the Spaniards and are defeated; a few survivors retreat to the mountains.

1518 The first African slaves are brought to Puerto Rico.

1539 Spanish colonists start building El Morro fortress.

1598 The English seize San Juan, the island's capital, and hold it for five months.

1625 Dutch sailors attack and burn San Juan.

1812 The constitution of 1812 guarantees Puerto Ricans basic civil rights.

1855 An outbreak of the disease cholera kills 20,000 Puerto Ricans.

1868 In the so-called El Grito de Lares uprising, revolutionary leader Ramón Emeterio Betances declares an independent Republic of Puerto Rico. The rebellion is soon crushed.

1898 The United States wins the Spanish-American War and takes control of Puerto Rico.

1900 The Foraker Act establishes a civil government in Puerto Rico.

1917 The Jones Act makes Puerto Ricans U.S. citizens.

1928 A hurricane devastates Puerto Rico's coffee and sugarcane plantations.

1932 Puerto Rican women win the right to vote.

1937 Nineteen people are killed in the Ponce Massacre, as police put a stop to a nationalist demonstration in that city.

1949 Luis Muñoz Marín becomes Puerto Rico's first elected governor.

1950 Two armed Puerto Rican nationalists attempt to assassinate President Harry Truman.

1952 Puerto Rico becomes a commonwealth.

1968 The New Progressive Party (PNP), which supports statehood, is formed.

1985 Heavy rains and flooding on the island cause two hundred deaths.

1993 Puerto Rico celebrates the five hundredth anniversary of Columbus's landing; Puerto Ricans vote to retain commonwealth status in a referendum.

1998 Hurricane Georges strikes Puerto Rico, causing $2 billion in damage.

2000 Puerto Ricans elect their first woman governor, Sila M. Calderón.

2003 The United States turns over its military base on Vieques to the Puerto Rican government.

2006 The government temporarily shuts down most government agencies to reduce spending.

2008 Luis G. Fortuño, Puerto Rico's representative in Congress, is elected governor.

2009 Puerto Rican-American Sonia Maria Sotomayor becomes the first Hispanic U.S. Supreme Court Justice.

ECONOMY

Agricultural Products: bananas, beef, coffee, milk, pineapples, sugar, tobacco

Manufactured Products: clothing, food products, electrical equipment, machinery, medicine, rum, scientific instruments

Mineral Resources: clay, copper, lime, nickel, sand, and gravel

Business and Trade: finance, health care, real estate, tourism, wholesale and retail trade

Pineapples

Coffee Harvest Festival At this February event in Maricao, you can look out over beautiful coffee plantations, see how coffee beans are roasted, and watch traditional *café con leche* (coffee with milk) being made.

Carnaval One of Puerto Rico's most festive parties usually falls in February in Ponce. For six days just before Lent, the Christian time of fasting before Easter, musicians and dancers parade through the streets wearing colorful costumes and papier-mâché masks.

Dulce Sueño Paso Fino Horse Show Puerto Rico showcases its special breed of Paso Fino horses in Guayama each March. Paso *fino* means "fine step," and the breed is known for giving an incredibly smooth ride.

Carnaval

Casals Festival

Sugar Festival In April San Germán throws a feast in honor of sugarcane, once the island's most important crop. Check out the cane-farming exhibitions and enjoy some local foods.

Danza Festival This weeklong festival in Ponce celebrates the *danza*, Puerto Rico's elegant ballroom dance. Beautifully dressed couples turn and sway to orchestra music on Plaza las Delicias.

Casals Festival Famous musicians from around the world come to San Juan to perform at this June festival, founded by the renowned Spanish cellist Pablo Casals, who moved to Puerto Rico in 1956.

San Juan Bautista Day Each May On June 21 San Juan throws a huge celebration for its patron saint, known in English as Saint John the Baptist. You can join the colorful processions in town or honor the saint in the traditional way, by walking backward three times into the sea.

Aibonito Flower Festival Brilliant roses, carnations, lilies, and begonias fill the little mountain town of Aibonito in June or early July. Visitors love to stroll past the flowers and breathe in their sweet perfume.

Fiesta de Santiago Apostol Puerto Rico shows off its African roots in this weeklong festival at the end of July in Loíza. Groups of drummers keep the beat as people in traditional costumes and masks dance for Santiago, Loíza's patron saint.

Jayuya Indigenous Festival In mid-November Jayuya celebrates the culture of Puerto Rico's early settlers. Visitors can enjoy traditional Taíno games, food, and music.

Bomba y Plena Festival Drummers, dancers, and singers gather in Ponce each November, filling the air with Puerto Rico's African-inspired *bomba* and *plena* music.

Hatillo Masks Festival On December 28 masked "devils" stalk the streets of Hatillo, pretending to be agents of King Herod, who ordered that all male infants be killed after Jesus was born.

Hatillo Masks Festival

COMMONWEALTH STARS

Julia de Burgos (1914–1953) was one of Puerto Rico's best-known poets. Like the Chilean poet Pablo Neruda who inspired her, she wrote about personal experiences, such as loneliness and love, as well as political subjects, like the need for freedom. In her most famous poem, "Río Grande de Loíza," she showed how the life of a person and a river intertwine. Burgos was born in Carolina.

José Campeche (1752–1809), Puerto Rico's first great painter, was also a talented musician, sculptor, and architect. His mother was a Spaniard from the Canary Islands, and his father, a former slave, was a master woodcarver. Campeche was born in San Juan. After studying painting there, Campeche produced close to four hundred portraits, religious pictures, and historical scenes, becoming one of Latin America's most respected artists. Campeche's paintings can be seen in many Puerto Rican churches.

Pablo Casals (1876–1973) was a celebrated cellist and conductor. Casals' musical talent blossomed when he was a young boy growing up in Spain. By the 1930s he was known the world over for his expressive cello music. In 1956 Casals moved to Puerto Rico, where his mother had been born. For the rest of his life he shared his passion for music with other people on the island. His presence is still felt during the Casals Festival in San Juan.

Roberto Clemente (1934–1972) was one of the best outfielders baseball has ever known. Clemente, who was born in Carolina, played with the Pittsburgh Pirates for seventeen years.

His powerful throwing arm won him twelve Golden Glove awards, and in 1966 he was named the National League's Most Valuable Player. Clemente died in a plane crash while trying to deliver supplies to the victims of an earthquake. He was inducted into the Baseball Hall of Fame in 1973.

Roberto Clemente

Ángel Cordero Jr. (1942–   ), a native of Santurce, is a champion jockey known for his competitive drive. Cordero's father and grandfather were also jockeys, and he started riding at age seventeen. A few years later he moved to New York, where he earned a reputation as a talented racer who could get his horses to give their all. By the time he retired at age fifty, Cordero had won more than seven thousand races, including three Kentucky Derbies, the most famous horse race in the United States.

José de Diego (1866–1921) was a brilliant poet and a founder of Puerto Rico's independence movement. A native of Aguadilla, Diego became active in politics as a young man. He helped start the Autonomist and Unionist political parties, both dedicated to giving Puerto Rico control over its own destiny. A talented speaker, journalist, and essay writer, he made a lasting mark on the literary world with his beautiful romantic poems.

José Feliciano (1945–   ) is a world-renowned singer and guitarist. Feliciano was born in Lares and moved to New York City with his family when he was five. Blind from birth, he taught himself music by listening to records. He first learned to play a small accordion and later the guitar.

José Feliciano

Over the years Feliciano's expressive voice and masterful guitar style have won him countless fans and six Grammy Awards. "Light My Fire" and "Feliz Navidad" are among his best-known songs.

Rosario Ferré (1938–) is a writer whose stories and novels address important Puerto Rican social issues. Ferré was born in Ponce and studied literature at the University of Puerto Rico. She founded and edited a magazine in the 1970s, and later wrote for the newspapers *El Nuevo Día* and the *San Juan Star*. Ferré's first novel, *Maldito Amor*, was published in 1988. Her other books include *La Casa de la Laguna* and *Vecindarios Excéntricos*.

Rafael Hernández (1892–1965) is the composer of some of Puerto Rico's best-loved popular songs. Hernández was born in Aguadilla and had a successful music career in both Puerto Rico and the United States. To many Puerto Ricans his ballads "Lamento Borincano," "Capullito de Alelí," and "Preciosa" are as much a symbol of the island as sandy beaches and palm trees.

Eugenio María de Hostos y Bonilla (1839–1903) was a leading teacher and social reformer. Born in Mayagüez, Hostos was an early supporter of Puerto Rican independence. He was educated in Spain, became a professor at the University of Chile, and helped reform the education system in the Dominican Republic. The author of many respected essays, Hostos became famous throughout Latin America both for his political views and for his graceful ability to express them.

Raul Juliá (1940–1994) was a successful stage and screen actor. A native of San Juan, Juliá fell in love with acting while playing the devil in a school play. In 1964 he gave his first New York performance, appearing in the Spanish production *La Vida es un Sueño* ("Life Is a Dream"). A natural performer, he later acted in everything from Shakespeare to musicals. Juliá also starred in a wide range of movies, including *Kiss of the Spider Woman* and *The Addams Family*.

Hector Lavoe (1946–1993) was the greatest salsa singer of the 1960s and 1970s. Born Hector Juan Pérez Martinez in Ponce, he arrived in New York City at age seventeen. Taking the stage name Lavoe (Spanish slang for "the voice"), he teamed up with trombonist Willie Colon and then sang with his own band. Lavoe attracted fans with his warm personality as well as with his amazing singing style. "Mi Gente" and "De Ti Depende" are two of his most popular songs.

Luis Llorens Torres (1878–1944) wrote beautiful poetry about what it means to be Puerto Rican. Llorens Torres was born in Juana Díaz, was educated in Spain, and later worked as a lawyer. In 1913 he helped found a literary magazine that took Puerto Rican poetry in a new direction. Llorens Torres was known as a *crollo* poet, which means he believed it was important to develop a special Puerto Rican style. One of his most celebrated poems is "Canción de las Antillas" ("Song of the Antilles").

Raul Juliá

Ricky Martin (1971–) is one of the world's most popular Latin music stars. Martin's good looks and great voice gave him a head start in the show business world. Born in San Juan, he started doing television commercials at age six and joined the teen singing group Menudo when he was twelve years old. In 1998 Martin shot to stardom with his hit single "La Copa de la Vita" from the album *Vuelve*, which earned him a Grammy Award. His hard-driving blend of rock, pop, and salsa has made him the best-selling Latin recording artist of all time.

Ricky Martin

Rita Moreno (1931–) is an actress who has helped expand the role of Hispanic women in show business. Born in Humacao, Moreno moved to New York when she was five years old. She was dancing on Broadway by the age of thirteen. During her acting career Moreno often had to play the part of the hot-tempered Latina, but her talent went far beyond that stereotype. In 1962 she won an Academy Award for her performance in *West Side Story*. She later acted in children's television, earning an Emmy Award for her work on *The Muppet Show*.

Rita Moreno

Luis Muñoz Marín (1898–1980), Puerto Rico's first elected governor, was an outstanding leader and a champion of the poor. The founder of the island's Popular Democratic Party, he worked to improve the lives of ordinary Puerto Ricans. Muñoz Marín served as governor from 1949 to 1965, was an author of Puerto Rico's constitution, and helped the island become a commonwealth in 1952. Muñoz Marín was born in San Juan and educated in Washington, D.C.

Luis Muñoz Marín

Juan "Chi Chi" Rodríguez
(1935–) is a professional golfer known for his flamboyant style. Rodríguez was born in Río Piedras, where his father eked out a living cutting sugarcane. As a young boy Juan used to practice his swing on tin cans instead of golf balls, using a club he made from the branch of a guava tree. Rodríguez rose to the top of professional golf in the 1960s. In 1979 he used part of his earnings to set up a foundation for troubled teens.

Juan "Chi Chi" Rodríguez

Tito Rodríguez (1923–1973) is a legend of New York's Latin music scene. Born in San Juan, Rodríguez moved to the United States in 1939 to sing in his brother's band. He rose to fame in the 1940s and 1950s when mambo, a big band style of Latin jazz, became popular. He led his own band starting in 1947, and for years he battled drummer Tito Puente for the title of Mambo King.

Luis Rafael Sánchez (1936–) is one of Puerto Rico's most respected writers. Sánchez was born in Humacao and studied theater at the University of Puerto Rico. His plays and novels are known for their rhythmic language, mixing everyday speech with older Spanish words. Sánchez writes most often about what it's like to be Puerto Rican. His novel *La Guaracha del Macho Camacho* (*Macho Comacho's Beat*), a comedy set in San Juan, brought him international acclaim.

Gilberto Santa Rosa (1962–), a native of San Juan, is known as the Gentleman of Salsa. Santa Rosa began studying music when he was twelve and sang with others before forming his own band. Santa Rosa is famous for improvising instead of singing his music the same way each time. In 1995 Santa Rosa became the first Puerto Rican salsa singer to perform at New York's Carnegie Hall.

Gilberto Santa Rosa

Félix Trinidad (1973–) is a boxer whose powerful punch is respected around the world. In 1993 he defeated two-time world champion Maurice Blocker to take the International Boxing Federation welterweight crown. By 2001 he had slugged his way to the World Boxing Association welterweight, super welterweight, and middleweight titles, and was still undefeated. Trinidad retired from boxing in 2005. He lives in Cupey Alto.

Félix Trinidad

Old San Juan (San Juan) Hundreds of pastel-colored buildings and shaded plazas make up the heart of Puerto Rico's capital.

Old San Juan

El Morro

El Morro (San Juan) It's great to watch the pounding surf from atop this 470-year-old fortress at the edge of San Juan Bay. You can also tour the secret tunnels behind its 20-foot-thick walls.

Río Camuy Cave Park (Lares) The Taíno Indians believed sacred spirits lived in this underground wonderland, one of the largest cave networks in the world. A highlight is the 170-foot-high Clara Cave.

Mona Island Just 45 miles from the main island of Puerto Rico, this island is full of wildlife, including sea turtles, iguanas, and more than a hundred species of birds.

Porta Coeli Church (San Germán) Built in 1606, this is the oldest church in the United States. The enormous doors are made of wood from the native ausubo tree.

El Yunque (Palmer) The Caribbean National Forest takes its nickname from the good Taíno spirit Yukiyú. Millions of tiny tree frogs called coquís are hidden among its ferns and palms.

Porta Coeli Church

Ponce Museum of Art

Ponce Museum of Art (Ponce) Paintings from Spain, Italy, Holland, France, Britain, and Puerto Rico are on display at this art museum, which claims to have the largest art collection in the Caribbean.

Las Cabezas de San Juan Nature Reserve

Las Cabezas de San Juan Nature Reserve (Fajardo) A guided tour of this
   protected stretch of coast will take you past coral reefs, mangrove forests,
   and quiet lagoons. A lighthouse stands on a 200-foot cliff above the sea.

San Juan Cathedral (San Juan) This ancient church contains explorer
   and first governor Juan Ponce de León's tomb.

Toro Negro Forest Reserve (Ponce) This forest surrounds Cerro de Punta, Puerto Rico's highest peak. The lush, rugged landscape is threaded with waterfalls.

Toro Negro Forest Reserve

Luquillo Beach (Luquillo) One of the island's most beautiful beaches lies in a crescent-shaped bay edged by a coconut grove.

Tropical Agriculture Research Station (Mayagüez) In these vast gardens you can see how local crops like cacao, yams, and bananas are grown.

Capilla del Cristo (San Juan) Statues of saints crowd this outdoor chapel next to the Parque de las Palomas. The silver ornaments the statues wear stand for healing miracles the saints are said to have performed.

Guánica Forest Reserve (Guánica) This landscape on the dry southwest side of Puerto Rico features many kinds of cactus and some of the island's most colorful birds.

Mosquito Bay (Vieques) When you pass through the waters of this bay at night, you leave a bright trail of light, cast by tiny underwater creatures that glow like fireflies.

Caguana Indian Ceremonial Park (Caguana) This shady park marks the ancient courts where Taíno Indians once played the ball game called *batey*. Some of the rocks that surround the courts are covered with Taíno drawings.

Museum of Puerto Rican Music (Ponce) Puerto Rican musical instruments of all kinds are on display here, including local favorites like the guiro and the maracas.

Luquillo Beach

Hacienda Buena Vista

Hacienda Buena Vista (Ponce) This mountainside farm was once a rich producer of coffee. The house and mill are preserved as they were in the 1800s, when crops were collected in giant bowls made from the root of the ceiba tree.

The flavoring ingredients for Coca-Cola and Pepsi are made in the town of Cidra.

Many words we use today are descended from the Taíno language, including hurricane, hammock, and canoe.

The deepest waters of the Atlantic Ocean are located just off Puerto Rico. About 75 miles north of the island is a depression of the seafloor called the Puerto Rico Trench. One end plunges into the Milwaukee Depth, where the ocean is more than 5 miles deep.

Find Out More

Would you like to learn more about Puerto Rico? You could start by checking your local library or bookstore for these titles.

GENERAL BOOKS

George, Marian M. *A Little Journey to Puerto Rico: For Intermediate and Upper Grades*. Teddington, UK: Echo Library, 2008.

Hernandez, Romel. *Puerto Rico* (The Caribbean Today). Broomall, PA: Mason Crest Publishers, 2008.

Stille, Darlene R. *Puerto Rico* (America the Beautiful, Third Series). New York: Children's Press, 2009.

SPECIAL INTEREST BOOKS

Bernier-Grand, Carmen and Lulu Delacre, illustrator. *Shake It, Morena! And Other Folklore from Puerto Rico*. Minneapolis, MN: Millbrook Press, 2006.

Hooper, Nancy and Raymond Betancourt, illustrator. *Everywhere Coquís! The Song of Puerto Rico*. Baltimore, MD: Omni Arts Publishers, 2007.

Worth, Richard. *Puerto Rico in American History* (From Many Cultures, One History). Berkeley Heights, NJ: Enslow Publishers, 2008.

FICTION

Jaffe, Nina and Enrique O. Sanchez, illustrator. *The Golden Flower: A Taíno Myth from Puerto Rico*. Houston, TX: Pinata Books, 2005.

MUSIC

Martin, Ricky. *17*. Sony International, 2008. The latest CD from Ricky Martin.

Puente, Tito. *The Essential Tito Puente*. RCA, 2005. A 2-CD box set from Tito Puente.

WEBSITES

Boricua Kids
www.elboricua.com/BoricuaKids.html
Loads of kid-friendly features on Puerto Rican food, history, people, and other topics can be found on this website.

DLTK's Crafts for Kids
www.dltk-kids.com/world/puerto_rico/
This fun website includes coloring pages, crafts, and puzzles, all having to do with Puerto Rico.

Time for Kids: Puerto Rico
www.timeforkids.com/TFK/teachers/aw/wr/main/0,28132,702661,00.
html
This is a kid-friendly website with fun facts from history, native lingo, geography, and much more.

The World Almanac for Kids
www.worldalmanacforkids.com/WAKI-ViewArticle.aspx?pin=wwwwak-432&article_id=777&chapter_id=15&chapter_title=United_States&article_title=Puerto_Rico
This encyclopedic site offers information on such topics as land and resources, history, and economy.

Index

Page numbers in **boldface** are illustrations and charts.

ABOUT THE AUTHORS

Martin Schwabacher is the author of more than twenty books for children, including *Minnesota* in the Celebrate the States series. He has also written for the American Museum of Natural History's exhibitions and websites. His research for *Puerto Rico* took him to every corner of the island, where he talked with many of the friendly people you will meet in this book.

Steve Otfinoski has written more than 130 books for children and young adults, including Marshall Cavendish's twelve-volume transportation series Here We Go! He is also the author of *New Hampshire* and *Georgia* in the Celebrate the State series.